For a year the miners fought to defend their jobs and **communities.** They took on the might of the British state. Their struggle **inspired** millions. This is their story.

Striking back

Photographs of the Great Miners' Strike 1984–1985

Title page photographs:
Top left: Santa being arrested for collecting toys for miners' children
Stefano Cagnoni/www.reportdigital.co.uk
Bottom left & right
John Sturrock/ Network Photographers

4

Striking Back: Photographs of the Great Miners' Strike 1984-1985

First published 2004
Bookmarks Publications Ltd,
c/o 1 Bloomsbury Street,
London WC1B 3QE.
Bookmarks, PO Box A338,
Sydney South, NSW 2000,
Australia.

ISBN
1 898876 51 7

Printed
Cambridge Printing

Words
Mike Simons

Design
John-Henry Barac

Acknowledgements
Hannah Dee
Paul Foot
Catriona Foote
Charlie Kimber
Paul McGarr
Ian Taylor
Alan Walter

Photographers

Stefano Cagnoni
Report Digital
www.reportdigital.co.uk
07860 864 363

John Harris
Report Digital
www.reportdigital.co.uk
07831 121 483
01789 262 151

Keith Pattison
mail@keithpattison.com

Martin Shakeshaft
www.martinshakeshaft.com
07899 997 237

John Sturrock
Network Photographers
07973 254 298

Andrew Wiard
www.reportphotos.com
07973 219 201

Many of the photographs in this book appeared in *Blood, Sweat and Tears*, a photographic record of the miners' strike

For information on the miners' continued fight for justice

NUM, Miners' Offices,
2 Huddersfield Road, Barnsley,
South Yorkshire S70 2LS.
Phone 01226 215 555

Women Against Pit Closures,
5 Darley Cliff Cottages,
Worsborough, Barnsley,
South Yorkshire S70 4AJ.

www.justiceformineworkers.com

www.minersadvice.co.uk

Contents

20 years on

Stefano Cagnoni/www.reportdigital.co.uk

6 Do you know of a strike involving 165,000 workers that lasted a year, and saw people killed on the picket line and others die scavenging for coal to keep warm? A struggle that saw 11,312 people arrested, 5,653 on trial, almost 200 held in prison and 960 sacked?

This is not a chapter from the history of Bolivia or apartheid South Africa. This was Britain in 1984-85, when the ruling class showed its true ruthlessness and contempt for democracy in its struggle to beat the miners.

Yet this was also a time of heroism and inspiration, of working class solidarity and initiative.

The miners' strike showed how ordinary people could take on those who control our world, and how they can change in the process. Women and men discovered new possibilities in their lives, new ideas and new horizons. They transformed their communities, and the lives of millions who supported them, even as they struggled to heat their homes and feed their children.

Tragically, their spirit was never matched for a moment by leaders of the Labour Party and trade unions, so the story of the miners' strike is also one of betrayal.

It began on 1 March 1984, when Margaret Thatcher and her government embarked on a naked class battle. They had come to power five years earlier determined to shift resources in British society decisively away from working people. They wanted to hack the welfare state, sell off state-owned industries such as coal mining, gas, electricity and telecommunications, and let market forces rip.

The Tories were trailblazers for global neo-liberalism. To achieve this they set out to destroy the power of the trade union movement, and in particular the National Union of Mineworkers – whose strikes in 1972 and 1974 had broken the previous Tory government.

Government economic policies drove official unemployment above 3 million and real unemployment to more than 4 million. The Tories put into practice the Ridley plan, a blueprint for taking on the unions devised by right wing MP Nicholas Ridley before the 1979 election.

This involved careful preparation before provoking a confrontation – bringing in anti-union laws, picking on the weaker unions first, cutting benefits to the families of strikers, and setting up mobile squads of police to smash pickets.

The government pushed through round after round of anti trade union legislation, which was met by only ineffectual protests by the union leaders. Ministers began a series of set-piece confrontations with individual groups of workers. They provoked a strike by steel workers. They took on civil servants, health workers, water workers and rail workers, and they banned trade unions at the GCHQ spy centre in Cheltenham in a calculated insult to the Trades Union Congress (TUC).

By 1984 the Tories had ridden out a wave of riots in the inner cities when angry youth fought back against mass unemployment and police racism. They had survived a mass peace movement led by the Campaign for Nuclear Disarmament in protest at the deployment of nuclear Cruise missiles on US bases in Britain.

After years of preparation, and having won a second election in 1983, Thatcher and her ministers felt ready to confront their most formidable enemy – the National Union of Mineworkers.

Coal was still the main source of energy for power stations and steel works. But the Tories prepared by building up coal stocks and ensuring docks could handle large-scale coal imports. They had oil-fired power stations taken out of mothballs and placed orders for oil far in advance, and they insisted creaking nuclear power stations be cranked up for action.

The Tories reorganised the police and had them trained to break strikes, and they appointed Ian MacGregor – whose life had been devoted to breaking unions around the world, and who had spent three years halving the workforce of the British Steel Corporation – as chair of the National Coal Board.

In March 1984 the government announced the closure of Cortonwood pit in South Yorkshire. This was the heart of the NUM's most militant area, and the pit had viable reserves of coal. But it would be just the first of 20 pit closures and 20,000 job

losses. The Tories had simply torn up the guarantees given by a previous government in the 1974 "A Plan for Coal", which followed two great strike victories by the miners.

If Cortonwood closed without a fight it would be a devastating blow to a union whose resistance already showed signs of weakening. Since 1981 NUM president Arthur Scargill had balloted his members for strikes against pit closures three times and been rejected.

The government knew that if the miners did not fight over Cortonwood and the other closures they never would. But no one could have imagined what was to follow. The Tories and the Coal Board calculated that any strike would be defeated within weeks. Instead, flying pickets from Cortonwood brought the rest of the huge Yorkshire coalfield to a standstill. Kent miners followed, and before long the coalfields of South Wales and Scotland were silent too.

Stunned by the spread of the strike, the Tories ordered thousands of police into the mining areas, while the media launched an unprecedented attack on the strikers and their leaders. In the most famous instance of this, the BBC re-edited film of a battle between miners and police at Orgreave in May 1984 to make it appear as though the pickets had launched an unprovoked attack on the police. In fact it was the other way round.

At least 165,000 miners went out on

strike. But up to 30,000 carried on working. Some people argued, and continue to argue, that the miners should have had a ballot before striking – this was in the days before ballots were compulsory. The Tories wanted a ballot because they hoped it would go against action and see the miners defeated. But some who said they backed the miners' case still argued in favour of a ballot and criticised the miners for not having one, claiming it would have unified the different areas in a way that picketing never could.

Neil Kinnock, the Labour Party leader at the time, has claimed his failure to call for the miners to ballot was the greatest political regret of his life.

But the call for a ballot was not a demand for genuinely democratic debate and decision-making. It was a weapon in a class war. When it suited governments they brushed aside ballots. In 1977, for example, the NUM conference and then the NUM members in a national ballot voted against an incentive scheme which led to different wages for miners in different parts of the country. The High Court ruled that the ballots were merely "advisory" and could be ignored. The government wanted the incentive scheme to divide the miners – which it did to great effect – so ballots went out of the window. In 1984 the miners' opponents wanted the ballot because they believed it would break the union.

In fact the 1984 strike spread to involve the great majority of the workforce through

We couldn't stand the TV making out that the wives weren't behind their men. Ten of us sat up half the night talking about what to do, and five of us decided to go and picket. We all said, "Thatcher wants to starve the miners back to work," so we all sat down and wrote out leaflets by hand, and distributed them through doors. Fifteen women came to the meeting, and we decided to set up the kitchen.

Isobel, Edlington, near Doncaster

9

a thoroughly democratic method – miners from one pit or area going to another to explain face to face why solidarity and unity were essential. It was not "thuggery" or "intimidation" which enabled Yorkshire miners to shut down Nottinghamshire pits in the early days of the strike. Some pits closed when as few as 30 pickets arrived.

In those early days the pickets set out as confidently as they had in 1972 and 1974. But the police were prepared, with some 11,000 specially trained and centrally controlled riot police. They had powers to stop pickets' cars and turn them back, to cordon off whole villages and areas, and to arrest people at will.

The strikers also discovered that they were to be much poorer than they had been in 1972 and 1974. The Tories had deducted £15 per week from the already desperately low benefits their families were entitled to. It seemed as though the mining communities must soon break under the pressure. But they did not.

For three months the pickets drove the strike forward. First they tried to bring out their fellow miners in Nottinghamshire. When only a minority of the Notts miners joined the strike, the pickets turned to economic targets – the giant steel works in Scotland, Wales and Yorkshire.

By the summer the miners had fallen back from the battles at the steel works to protect their own heartlands. The government, believing it had the upper hand, scuppered peace talks. Yet as the strike became a grim war of attrition, the strikers seemed to gain a new spirit, a new strength.

Life was different. The daily grind of shift working and days underground was gone. Instead life revolved around decisions about picketing, fundraising and welfare, and discussions about the political ebb and flow of the strike.

People changed. They felt a new confidence in themselves and those around them, and this led to changes in the way they behaved towards one another. Deeply ingrained ideas and prejudices crumbled.

Mining was virtually an all-male industry. But women came to the fore, and ideas about women's liberation flourished in the

Martin Shakeshaft

day to day battle to survive. The communal kitchens run by women became the heart and soul of the strike. The most energetic and forceful of the many miners' support groups were driven almost exclusively by women.

Women activists and trade unionists beyond the pit villages challenged the sexism of many miners while delivering support on a scale never seen before by the British working class. The process led to new relationships in the mining communities and in the home – to new uncertainties, but also to new respect.

The strike challenged other prejudices. There were few black or Asian people in the mining communities, but the support the miners received from black, Asian and immigrant communities saw miners who held racist ideas reassess their views.

Similarly, anti-gay attitudes had been prevalent in many mining communities. But these were challenged as gays and lesbians became involved in supporting the strike. In London a group called Lesbians and Gays Support the Miners collected thousands of pounds for miners in South Wales and bought the strikers a minibus. The group visited mining areas and discussed gay oppression with a community that was itself under attack.

The experience began to change attitudes, to the extent that after the strikers returned to work a delegation of miners led the 1985 Gay Pride march through London.

The strike also turned many of the socialist slogans on the miners' lodge banners into a physical reality – an injury to one was an injury to all, the strong did help the weak.

But the impact extended way beyond the mining areas to every workplace, shopping centre, school and college. Black on yellow "Coal not dole" stickers blossomed everywhere.

At the start of the strike donations were collected by union officials and sent off to a national fund. By late autumn 1984 most donations were going to individual pits through the "twinning" of trade union branches, student unions and even street committees with NUM branches and pit villages. Miners and their families travelled out of their communities, and supporters from outside moved in. New friendships sprouted.

Through August, September and October the strike held solid. For a time, as the TUC promised to mobilise solidarity action, the government wavered. The miners could still have won then and saved us from 13 more years of the Tories. But the promised support failed to materialise.

While the TUC dithered, the Tories and the Coal Board chiefs called in shadowy friends to organise a "back to work movement". Tim Bell, an adviser to the prime minister and managing director of the Tories' favourite advertising agency, Saatchi and Saatchi, took over anti-strike advertising for the Coal Board.

Hands off our pits!

HANDS OFF

OUR UNION!

Hands off our people!

David Hart, a right wing property tycoon, was authorised to start and fund a "Working Miners' Committee" from the dregs of the strikebreakers. In four days of advertising in Tory papers Hart's "committee" raised more than £100,000. Other newspapers and the television joined the growing campaign to push the miners back to work.

Coal Board executives predicted an end to the strike by Christmas. But the miners and their supporters redoubled their efforts. The support groups mobilised to ensure every miner's child enjoyed their Christmas.

As the new year began, after nine months on strike, there were still 130,000 miners out. Their strike was costing the government up to £50 million a week.

But the bitter cold of January did not bring the power cuts the miners needed. The nuclear and oil-fired power stations, operated at full blast, could power homes and industries as long as the crucial 50,000 tons of coal a week came in from Nottingham.

Instead the cold added to the hardship of the strikers, and increasing numbers began to drift back to work.

By the first week of March the flow back to work had become too strong. The strikers were finally being starved back to work. So they went back together, heads held high, after being on strike for a year – the longest mass strike in British, European or US history.

The end of the strike produced an inevitable backlash. Those like Labour leader Neil Kinnock who denounced "picket line violence", and the trade union leaders who promised support but delivered little, spread a series of myths about the strike.

They said it was a mistake – that it would have been better if the strike had never happened, that it was all the fault of "extremists" such as Arthur Scargill, that it would have been better to have had a ballot and lost than to have gone through a "year of hell" for nothing.

These arguments are repeated today by politicians, professors and media pundits. Strikes, pickets, protests and demonstrations are old fashioned, they say, and change can only come through the ballot box. Yet we had to wait more than a decade after the strike to be rid of the Tories through the ballot box – only to be left asking how much has really changed between the days of Thatcher and New Labour.

Although they did not win, the miners stopped the Thatcher government in its tracks. It cost the Tories more than £7

Strikers outside NUM special conference, Sheffield, 19 April 1984
John Sturrock/Network Photographers

12 billion to defeat the strike, and it was several years before they dared launch another all-out attack on the miners.

The lessons are important for today. The struggle was not lost because it was led by left wingers or because the miners did not hold a ballot. The miners were forced back to work because the other side was better organised and prepared.

The strike showed the government, police, courts, big business and media in their true light, while exposing the untrustworthiness of leaders of the trade unions and Labour Party.

At the same time, it showed that millions can be galvanised by a battle to put people before profits, and that solidarity can defy seemingly overwhelming odds.

The photographs gathered here give a glimpse of the story. They demonstrate the power of organised workers confronting the government, and show the values around which the strike was fought.

Those values – that we don't have to bow to market forces, that ordinary people can transform themselves and their communities when they unite against the ravages of free market capitalism – have never been more relevant.

This is not a book about a glorious defeat – it is about a defeat that was not inevitable. It has a simple aim – to inspire the activists in the anti-globalisation and anti-war movements, and the new generation of militants emerging in the trade unions, to avenge the miners' defeat.

Here we go

The Thatcher government provoked the miners' strike on its terms and at a time of its choosing. No miner would have chosen to go on strike in the spring and with coal stocks high.

But on 1 March 1984 the National Coal Board announced the closure of Cortonwood colliery in South Yorkshire, and warned that 20 more pits would close within a year, threatening 20,000 jobs.

George Robertson, secretary of the Cortonwood branch of the National Union of Mineworkers, understood exactly what was happening: "Cortonwood had a reputation as a moderate pit. For several years it had taken workers from other pits that had closed. Cortonwood suited Maggie's purpose, and they planned to provoke us. She thought we wouldn't strike, and she thought we wouldn't get support. She was wrong."

In Yorkshire hundreds of miners packed halls in clubs. Everyone backed the strike. The atmosphere was one of elation. A confrontation with the government had finally arrived. Hundreds of men put their names down for picketing, aiming to present their arguments for action face to face with fellow miners whose jobs might be on the line in a year or two.

While the media focussed on Wales and Scotland – where many miners were demoralised by recent failures to prevent pit closures, local votes were going against the strike – pickets were already travelling the country spreading the action.

Jack Collins, a senior NUM official in Kent, had this to say: "The fight came from the bottom, not the leadership...the only tactic we need is to let the men develop the strike... If the miners are determined to stop work then that determination should be directed not only into their own coalfields but others as well."

In Scotland and South Wales, miners from pits which backed the strike picketed those that did not. Within 36 hours both coalfields were at a standstill. From Yorkshire, miners were already crossing the border into Nottinghamshire, where the area's NUM leaders had refused to back the strike without a ballot. For the first 48 hours the flying pickets were well received by their fellow miners and there was little violence.

Whenever rank and file miners argued with their fellow workers about the need to unite and fight, they were generally successful. The government was left horrified as shift after shift at pits in north Nottinghamshire refused to cross the Yorkshire miners' picket lines.

Fearful that the Nottinghamshire miners would join the Yorkshire men on strike, Thatcher ordered the police into action while the media whipped up a campaign

Ten storeys up, Arthur Scargill is telling 3,000 miners lobbying the NUM executive that there will be no retreat. The miners were delighted – the government horrified, Sheffield, 12 April 1984
John Sturrock / Network Photographers

We've got to have mass pickets because it's the only way we can counter the press and present the arguments about pit closures.

Armthorpe miner

Below left: The first Yorkshire pickets at Bevercotes colliery, Notts, 12 March 1984
John Sturrock/Network Photographers

Right: Mass picket of the night shift at Ollerton, Notts, 14 March 1984. Yorkshire miner David Jones died after being hit by a brick thrown at this picket line
John Sturrock/Network Photographers

16 against "picket line violence".

The *Financial Times* described the scene in Downing Street: "Mrs Thatcher is understood to be angered by the failure of the police to prevent these disturbances. She is believed to have banged the table while making critical remarks about some chief constables."

Some 8,000 police were dispatched into the Nottinghamshire pit villages. At Ollerton the police made their first attempts to prevent the Yorkshire pickets talking to Notts miners. The violence they provoked was to become the hallmark of the strike. It was at Ollerton that the first victim of the strike, David Jones – a young Yorkshire miner – was killed by a brick thrown at the pickets.

After David Jones's death the Tory home secretary spelled out the government's interpretation of the law on picketing: "Police have the power to stop their [miners'] vehicles on the road and turn them away. Anyone not complying would be committing a criminal offence."

For the next three weeks pickets engaged in a cat and mouse game with police as they tried to picket the pits.

Miners and their supporters were pulled up by police on motorway slip roads miles from any picket line and told they faced arrest unless they turned back.

More than 150 miles from the Nottinghamshire coalfield, police stopped Kent miners travelling north through the

Dartford Tunnel on pain of arrest. In Nottinghamshire mining villages police imposed a curfew and identity checks, and dished out beatings to striking miners and Yorkshire pickets.

The government's interpretation of the law, and the actions of the police in Nottinghamshire, drove the right wing chief constable of Greater Manchester, James Anderton, to tell the *Daily Mail*, "The police have imposed a kind of curfew on the community as a whole, not just on the miners, and have restricted free movement. These features are things we normally only associate with countries behind the Iron Curtain. The police are getting the image of a heavy-handed mob" (31 March 1984).

As the police strove to isolate the Nottinghamshire coalfield, the media launched a furious propaganda campaign, centred on the demand for a national strike ballot.

This sought to portray the strike as undemocratic and isolate those fighting to defend jobs from the rest of the trade union movement. It also provided an excuse for those miners' leaders who did not want to take on the Tories.

But the NUM already had a mandate for action against pit closures. With 80 to 90 percent of the membership on strike, the NUM's national leaders did not need another one. Nottinghamshire became the only area of any significance in which a majority of miners remained at work.

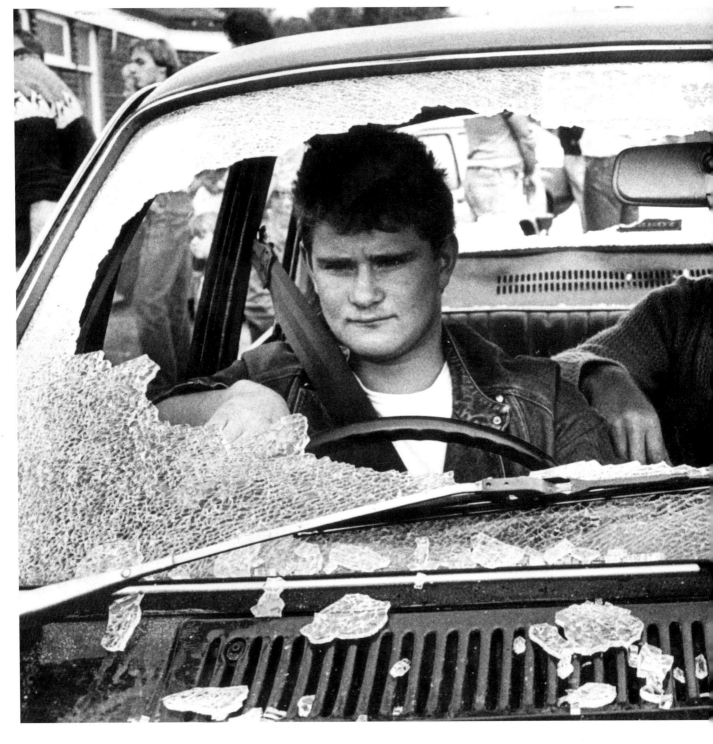

The chief constable of Nottinghamshire, Mr Charles McClachlan, denied police officers used a crowbar to smash the windscreen of a picket's car. It was, he said, a truncheon.

Financial Times, *March 1984*

We are determined to ensure mass picketing is not permitted

David Hall, chief constable of Humberside and controller of the National Reporting Centre

Only 100 Yorkshire miners broke through the police surveillance to picket the 25 Nottinghamshire pits

Guardian *reports on the effectiveness of the blockades, 28 March 1984*

Barnsley miners after police smash windscreen at a roadblock at Cuckney crossroads, Nottinghamshire
John Harris/ www.reportdigital.co.uk

We've got to step up the tempo of the dispute. I want to see every single miner on strike on the picket line. If that means you get arrested, you'll have to accept the consequences. We're in this to the finish.

Arthur Scargill speaking before he joined the picket line

Above: Scargill calls for more pickets, Ollerton, 27 April 1984
John Sturrock/Network Photographers

Right: 40,000 striking miners march in Mansfield, heart of the only major working coalfield, 14 May 1984
John Sturrock/Network Photographers

Orgreave: the turning point

"The phoney war is over. The real struggle, the most profound and serious labour challenge to have faced the Thatcher government, has begun."

Financial Times, 7 April 1984.

With the overwhelming majority of miners out on strike, the establishment braced itself for unprecedented confrontation. Both sides agreed on one thing – the miners could only succeed if the union was able to hit the industries which depended on coal.

There were record coal stocks at the power stations, where the miners' strikes of the 1970s had been won. The steel plants were the government's weakness, and it was steel which provided the battleground this time.

By the end of March 1984 production was already being cut back at some of the UK's giant steel works in a bid to conserve coal. On 28 March the *Financial Times* reported that some plants might shut down without fresh supplies. This would, in turn, hit the motor and engineering industries.

It was a chance for the miners to have a real impact, but the opportunity was thrown away. While the NUM's national leaders and the pickets concentrated on making the strike bite, officials of the NUM in Scotland, Yorkshire and Wales

Miners from all the striking coalfields formed the last mass picket at Orgreave, 18 June 1984
John Sturrock/Network Photographers

reached agreements with the steel unions to supply coal to local plants.

The area leaders thought they were supplying just enough to prevent the steel works closing – since they worried that, once shut, the plants would never be reopened. But they had been conned. The agreements did not merely keep the plants open and limit output. They undermined the strike by maintaining levels of steel production.

On 27 April 1984 miners and rail union leaders in Scotland agreed to restrict supplies to Ravenscraig steel works to one train of coal each day. The British Steel Corporation responded by carrying coal in convoys of lorries to Ravenscraig. The subsequent battles between pickets and police failed to stop the convoys. Eventually a deal allowed enough coal to ensure production at Ravenscraig.

In Yorkshire the poor quality of available coking coal was affecting production at the Scunthorpe steel works. The British Steel Corporation again decided to use convoys of lorries, this time to carry good quality stocks from the Orgreave coking plant, near Rotherham, to Scunthorpe. As the convoys rolled, moving coal from under the noses of picketing miners, local militants were quick to react.

Orgreave saw the bloodiest confrontations in any industrial dispute since before

Orgreave, 30 May 1984
John Sturrock/Network Photographers

Left: Lesley Boulton, a member of
Sheffield Women's Support
Group, calling for an ambulance
for a nearby injured miner.
18 June 1984
John Harris/www.reportdigital.co.uk

Below: Orgreave May 1984
John Sturrock/Network Photographers

28 the First World War. It revealed class warfare at its most naked. For the miners, Orgreave was a chance to turn the tide – a chance to hit an economic target and provide a focus around which other trade unionists could mobilise support.

For the government, with its legions of riot police, Orgreave was a chance to show to the miners and trade unionists at large that picketing could not succeed.

From the end of May through to mid-June miners and police engaged in a series of increasingly violent confrontations at Orgreave. But despite the wishes of rank and file miners, the NUM's area leaders never called mass pickets at Orgreave for more than two consecutive days. As a result, it was impossible for them to rally massed ranks of local engineering and steel workers in support, as the pickets in 1972 had done at the Saltley coke depot in Birmingham, in the decisive battle of that strike.

Instead, the miners were alone when they tried to prevent convoys of lorries taking coking coal from Orgreave to Scunthorpe. They faced police baton charges and mounted police wielding riot sticks.

One picket summed up the police tactics: "They were out to maim, not to arrest." Another said, "There weren't many arrests [at Orgreave]. People got arrested when they went to hospital. One lad was surrounded by horses and beaten to the ground. I tried to talk him into going to hospital. But when we got there we were

We have to make it clear that violence is totally unaccceptable in our society

Margaret Thatcher, Tory Party women's conference, 23 May 1984

This is so untypical and so un-British

Neil Kinnock attacks the miners after Orgreave

30   told not to go in – they were arresting injured miners."

The last battle at Orgreave was on 18 June 1984, when 5,000 pickets in T-shirts and trainers confronted a similar number of police with riot shields, backed by dogs and horses. Overwhelmed by the scale of police violence, the pickets were called off.

The government knew it had won an important round, and broke off negotiations with the NUM. The *Economist* magazine noted, "The government wants to be seen to have broken the legendary power of the miners."

The events at Orgreave provoked bitter arguments. Some miners' leaders subsequently argued that mass pickets could never succeed against paramilitary-style policing.

But many rank and file NUM activists argued that the failure at Orgreave came because the union did not organise consistent picketing, day after day, that could act as a beacon for other workers to rally round.

Arthur Scargill believed the latter argument was correct. After area leaders signalled an end to picketing at Orgreave he said, "Some people say that the problem was a failure of mass picketing, but I say it was a failure to mass picket."

Now the miners faced a war of attrition, as the Tories and Coal Board tried to starve them back to work, and the miners tried to hold on until winter and the expected power cuts.

Left: Orgreave, 18 June 1984
John Harris/www.reportdigital.co.uk

Below: Orgreave, June 1984
Martin Shakeshaft

The government...decided to use the "thin blue line" as its battering ram against Arthur Scargill...the police service has unwittingly allowed itself to be portrayed as Margaret Thatcher's puppets.

Inspector Peter Bartlett, letter to the Guardian

Left: Orgreave,
June 1984
Martin Shakeshaft

Right: Back page of a
special issue of the
Miner, journal of the
NUM, 2 June 1984

Published by the National Union of Mineworkers, St. James' House, Vicar Lane, Sheffield. Printed by Trader Web Offset Limited, Heanor Gate Estate, Heanor, Derbyshire. Tel: 0773 717331.

33

**We were faced with the
alternative…either stop mass
picketing at the time or lose the
initiative completely. The closure
of Orgreave might have been the
start of a lot of closures.**

*Tony Clements, assistant chief constable,
South Yorkshire*

Solidarity and support

The government, the police, the Coal Board and the media turned up the pressure on the miners and their families after Orgreave. Thousands of miners were arrested and hundreds jailed. Many more were released on bail conditions that prevented them being active in the strike. Social security rules were applied ever more stringently, while miners and their supporters collecting money in the streets suffered police harassment.

Speaking to Tory MPs in July 1984, Thatcher made plain she was fighting a class war, declaring, "We had to fight an enemy without in the Falklands. We always have to be aware of the enemy within, which is more dangerous."

The mining communities were tasting the full power of a state machine geared to crush them. But the government had reckoned without the organising power of women. Mines are not just places where men work. They sustain whole communities, and it was the women of those communities who drew together and set about the task of sustaining the strike.

They took strength not only from their own history and the memory of the strike kitchens of the 1920s, but from the lessons of the modern women's movement.

Women who had seldom stirred outside their local communities found themselves addressing meetings up and down the country, and travelling abroad in search of support. Their confidence grew as they organised, as did their sense of rage and injustice. They picketed, marched and lobbied, as well as feeding, clothing and supporting their men, their children and each other. They gave the strike a new heart, and transformed their own lives in the process.

Gradually yellow badges on lapels proclaiming support for the miners spread across the country. People rallied around the strikers and women's action groups. Support committees blossomed to organise union collections, street collections, food collections, benefit concerts, socials and bingo sessions. Workers abroad responded, too. French and Danish trade unionists sent shiploads of foodm and miners' children took free holidays abroad.

While the Tories imported coal from Russia and Poland, Solidarnosc – the independent trade union fighting Poland's military regime – sent a message of support. As the Tories imported coal from apartheid South Africa, black South African miners organised collections for the NUM. In Australia dockers and seafarers refused to handle coal bound for Britain, and in Denmark dockers fought a pitched battle with riot police to stop coal being

Women show Thacher they won't be used to undermine the strike, Maerdy, Rhonda Valley, South Wales, August 1984
Martin Shakeshaft

A rally organised by Blackburn Trades Council raised a magnificent £1,100. Miners were impressed to see that the biggest donation, of £250, came from the Asian community.

Hem Heath colliery newsletter, 18 June 1984

exported to undermine the strike.

Yet even while this solidarity grew, trade union leaders in Britain were busy undermining it. A series of days of action called by regional TUCs was condemned by TUC general secretary Len Murray. While rail workers stood firm in supporting the miners and refused to move coal trains, the Transport and General Workers Union failed to stop its lorry driver members running coal and coke into the steel plants.

A two-week dock strike in the summer delivered the first real setback to the government. But dockers' leaders failed to build the strike into a second front against the Tories. At one point the pit deputies' union, Nacods, looked set to join the strike after the Coal Board ripped up a series of agreements with the union. Had the pit deputies walked out, all coal production would have stopped. Instead their leaders reached a deal that once again left the striking miners isolated.

Each time a group of workers took action alongside the miners the Tories began to panic and reopened negotiations on a settlement. When the miners were left to fight alone the government pulled the rug from under talks.

Through the summer of 1984 trade union leaders veered between making statements condemning picket line violence and half-hearted pledges of solidarity. At the same time, some trade union members were putting their jobs on the

Left: Australian seaferers at Tilbury docks hand
over 800 Australian dollars from the crew to
striking Kent miners, 21 September 1984
Stefano Cagoni/www.reportdigital.co.uk

Below: CGT miners from the Pas du Nord
coalfield brought food and money to the strikers
John Sturrock/Network Photographers

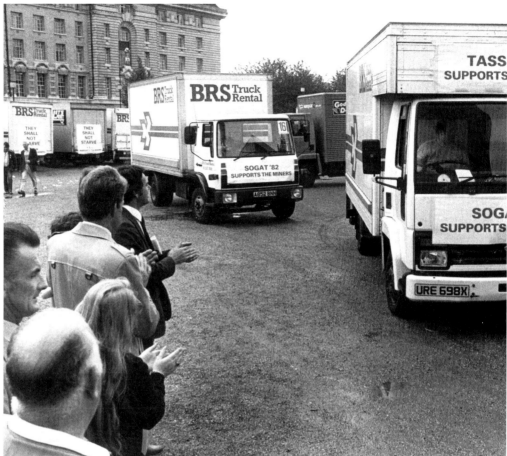

Left: Women in Cardiff protest
Martin Shakeshaft

Right: £100,000 convoy of food sets off for Barnsley miners' families, London, 2 August 1984. Trade unionists on Britain's national papers collected an estimated £2 million for the miners during the strike
Stefano Cagnoni/ www.reportdigital.co.uk

line and many more were digging deep in their pockets to support the miners.

At Coalville, in the middle of the working Leicestershire coalfield, no coal was moved by rail for 35 weeks.

At the *Sun*, print union workers refused to handle a front page which likened Arthur Scargill to Hitler, and then closed the paper down for three days when the management refused to publish a half-page statement by them in support of the miners.

As the strike dragged on, millions of workers watching the almost daily police assaults on the picket lines recognised the miners were fighting a battle for the future of the trade union movement.

There isn't a pit village in this country where there isn't a women's support group of some kind. We've been on rallies together, raised money together, and sometimes even cried together. But one thing we are determined to do is stick together for as long as this strike lasts.

Janine, Normanton

Far left top:
Lobby of TUC, 3
September 1984
*John Sturrock/
Network Photographers*

Far left bottom:
Women picket Tory
Party conference
Martin Shakeshaft

Top left:
Miners' wives show
their disgust at media
coverage of the
strike. National
miners' wives'
demonstration,
London, 11 August
1984
*John Harris/
www.reportdigital.co.uk*

Bottom left:
Coventry colliery
women outside the
NCB
*John Sturrock/
Network Photographers*

Right:
Electricians show
solidarity with miners
as demonstration
passes through Fleet
Street
*Andrew Wiard/
www.reportphotos.com*

**In all the places in London
Transport where we've taken
miners they've had the most
fantastic reception. I'll give one
example. We asked for a pair of
shoes for one child in Bentley pit
in Yorkshire – and we were given
40 pairs. If we build up the human
content of the strike by building
direct contact between the
miners and people in workplaces
it helps us build our own
organisation.**

Alan Watts, AUEW

State of siege

The government did not simply wait for the collapse of the strike after Orgreave. It sought to engineer a drift back to work. Thatcher wanted a humiliating defeat for the miners and for picketing.

Millionaire David Hart, an aide of both Thatcher and MacGregor, established a National Working Miners' Committee. A series of legal actions against the NUM in the committee's name culminated in the seizure of the union's funds and the appointment of a Receiver.

The press tried to make a hero out of a blacksmith from Bevercotes colliery called Chris Butcher, whom it christened "Silver Birch". Butcher promised to lead a mass return to work, and boasted of his financial backers to the *Mail on Sunday*: "Wealthy business people who want the strike to finish."

Then the government launched a propaganda offensive, claiming the strike was only held together by fear and intimidation. This provided a cover for moving the police into the core striking coalfields. The police invaded the villages. Sometimes they came to get a single scab back into work. At others they arrived on a purely punitive raid. As summer turned to autumn, more and more villages were on the receiving end. Those who had thought the

The pickets are at the pit, the shops are open, and the riot police move in, 4am, Grimethorpe, near Barnsley, October 1984
John Sturrock/Network Photographers

stories of police brutality at Orgreave far-fetched now saw for themselves. In Fitzwilliam, near Pontefract, squads of police descended on a pub just before closing time, ostensibly to pick up a man suspected of "vandalism". Lord Gifford, who defended those arrested at the subsequent trial, described what happened:

"Fifty police officers charged into the area on the double, with no warning, synchronised in a pincer movement... They entered private property without the invitation or consent of the landlord... It was a police riot. A punitive expedition by a newly arrived chief inspector determined to stamp his authority on the community."

The intimidation did not stop with the police. Courts in the mining areas added their stamp to the siege. Miners charged with picketing or other offences, however trivial, were confined to their villages, placed under curfew or had their movements restricted as a routine part of bail conditions.

The siege of the mining villages was accompanied by some of the most cynical news manipulation of the entire strike. Journalists who got no closer to a picket line than a police press conference would report a police briefing as fact, while the occupation of mining communities went unreported. The lies finally became too much for print workers at the *Sun*. They stopped the paper when, after a pitched battle at Silverwood colliery in South Yorkshire, an editorial denounced miners as

This lad went into the garden – he was running but jumping from foot to foot to avoid the flowers. The copper following him went straight through the lot. It's not their village, you see. They don't care.

Easington villager

The British police do not have sophisticated riot equipment to handle demonstrations. The traditional approach is to deploy large numbers of officers in ordinary uniform in the passive containment of a crowd. Neither the government nor the police wish to see this approach abandoned in favour of more aggressive methods.

Government Green Paper

Police horses charge mass picket at Brodsworth colliery, near Doncaster, 12 October 1984
John Sturrock/Network Photographers

Final police charge at
Broadsworth, 12 October 1984
John Sturrock/Network Photographers

"the scum of the earth".

The mining communities did fight back. Whole communities came onto the streets to defend themselves, to show it was possible to defy the police, the government and the pillorying of the press.

Pit villages such as Easington in County Durham were occupied by thousands of riot police intent on forcing strikebreakers through picket lines. Billy Stobbs, chair of the local NUM branch, said, "I've lived in Easington all my life and never thought in my wildest dreams I would see police baton-charge workers fighting for their jobs."

Heather Woods, one of the organisers of the Easington soup kitchens, said, "My kids now call the police 'pigs'. I didn't teach them. They have seen what has happened and they have learnt it for themselves. I used to see, on television, kids in Northern Ireland treating police like this and thought the parents must be to blame. Now I see you don't need to indoctrinate them. The police do it for them." The film *Billy Elliot* gives a taste of events in Easington, where it was set.

In Grimethorpe, South Yorkshire, police with riot shields attacked men, women and children scavaging for coal among spoil from the colliery. As news of the attacks spread, miners responded by first picketing and then attacking lorries that the union had allowed to take coal from the pit. For the next two days there was guerrilla warfare in the village.

The heat was only taken out of the confrontation when the South Yorkshire Police Committee called a pubic meeting to let residents have their say.

"I've been assaulted, kicked, punched and handcuffed," said Grimethorpe mayor Norman Whittaker. Miner's wife Elaine Crawford told of trying to stop the police "kicking hell" out of a young boy and being told, "Get home, you whore." The chairman of the police committee likened some of the police in Grimethorpe to "Nazi stormtroopers". Frank Gutsell, the assistant chief constable of South Yorkshire, told the meeting, "I apologise, apologise unreservedly."

The events in Easington and Grimethorpe were repeated up and down the coalfields. But when the mining communities fought against the scabs and their police escorts they found their resistance denounced by both Labour and TUC leaders who used the press hysteria about violence to hide their shame at not delivering the support promised at the TUC and Labour Party conferences.

The defiance of the communities shattered the Tory and Coal Board hopes that a single scab at any pit, brought in under massive police escort, could act as a magnet for others. Far from attracting more miners to break the strike, the scabs attracted more people to the picket lines.

It also showed the government would be hard-pressed to move pithead coal stocks to the power stations. Instead it had to use oil to maintain the power supplies, running up a bill of £2 billion in the process.

Left: A 13 year old boy is arrested after police attack coal pickers on a colliery waste tip, Grimethorpe, 17 Ocotber 1984
John Harris/ www.reportdigital.co.uk

Top right: Police with dogs patrol at night, Kellingley colliery, Pontefract, Yorkshire, 14 January 1985
John Sturrock/ Network Photographers

Bottom right: Ian Wright, a member of Hammersmith Miners' Support Committee, visited the picket line at Maltby. He was standing at the rear of the picket when the police attacked, 24 September 1984
John Sturrock/ Network Photographers

Right: Josie Smith, a disabled miner, arbitrarily accused of following scabs and arrested while standing outside his back gate, Easington, February 1985
Keith Pattison

Below: Darrel Price is carried into an ambulance after the police attack a mass picket, Rossington, 17 October 1984
John Harris/www.reportdigital.co.uk

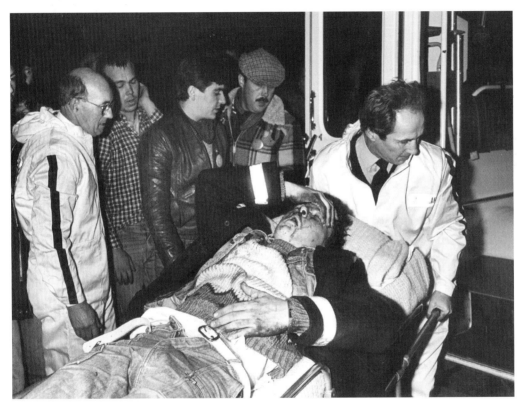

The police horse box accelerated and swerved towards a group of pickets. Darrel got hit. I thought he was dead. Another two feet and he would have gone right under the wheels. Some lads went over to the police as he lay seriously injured, and all they did was laugh. They started chanting, "We hope he's dead." They wouldn't call an ambulance.

Wath upon Dearne miner

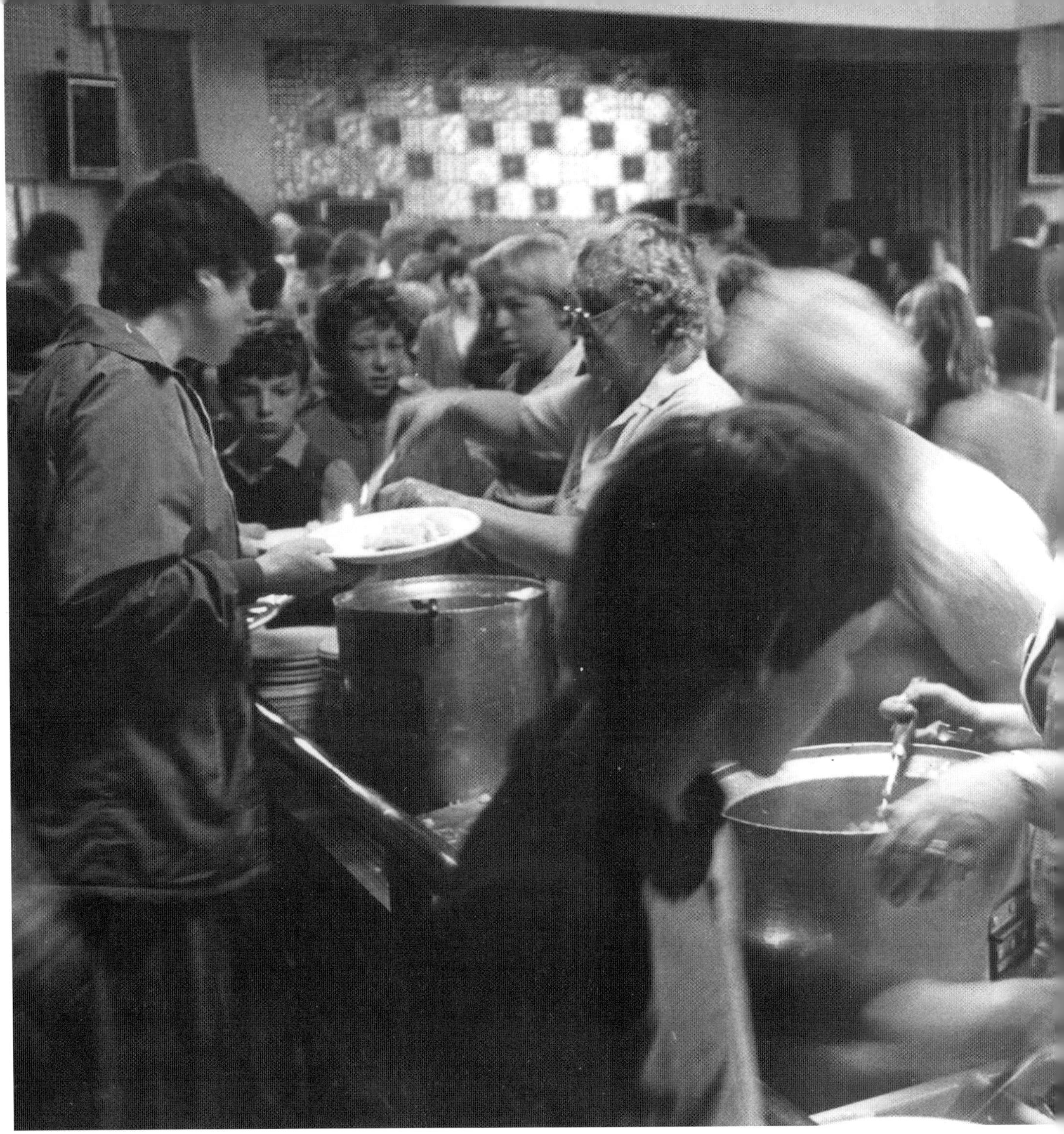

Holding on

Easington kitchen and strike centre, Durham, August 1984
Keith Pattison

Throughout the autumn the Tories grew desperate to crack the strike. They did not know whether they could get through the winter without power cuts, and every week the miners stayed out cost them millions.

They continued to underestimate the resilience of the strike and the deep well of support it tapped into.

The mining communities were thrown back on their own resources. Teams of miners searched local woods for dead and dying trees to cut for fuel. The kitchens expanded to provide one square meal a day for anyone who needed it. Outside the communities there was an increasing sense of urgency in the miners' support groups.

The practice of twinning a trade union branch with a soup kitchen or NUM branch spread rapidly. Sometimes there seemed no logic to it. Print union branches in Fleet Street would twin with tiny groups of strikers in Nottinghamshire. Some pits in the Doncaster area twinned with local authority trade unionists in a London borough.

Folks said at the start of the strike that they'd manage without the food kitchen. They didn't want to go back to those days. But they're here now. Every week there are new families turning up needing feeding.

Maureen Walsh, Hatfield, from the newsletter of Nupe members in Camden, north London

This could provide a weekly income many times that of the next-door pit, yet somehow the money was shared around. Nottinghamshire strikers took tons of donated food up to the Northumberland and Durham coalfields. In Yorkshire "twinned" kitchens bailed out those in neighbouring villages.

Support groups flourished across the UK, as two activists in the support movement explained in early 1985:

"On Merseyside there are 14 support groups, which have between them sent over £1 million – not including workplace collections – and new groups are still being formed. There are normally 50 to 60 miners out in the city centre.

"From Birmingham support goes to South Wales, and has also gone to more local coalfields. From London it has gone to Kent, South Wales, Staffordshire and the north east. Individual boroughs and support groups have twinning arrangements with pits in many different coalfields. There are people with buckets and collections of food on high streets everywhere, an anarchy of support groups."

Twinning created a bond between the mining villages and their supporters. There was constant traffic between the pit villages and major towns. Teams of collectors and speakers would be despatched from the villages, returning with delegations of trade unionists, socialists and Labour Party activists. Stunned by the hardship they witnessed, and overwhelmed by the generos-

ity and spirit they encountered, the visitors would return home determined to do more. The impact on the villages was enormous. Every visitor helped overcome the feeling of isolation and hopelessness the government was trying to instil. Every pound collected allowed the strikers to survive another day. In the autumn and winter of 1984 lasting friendships were forged between mining families and their supporters.

But the struggle brought tragedy, too. On 5 November 1984 Erick Knapper, a 38 year old father of two from Sharleston colliery in North Yorkshire, died while picking for waste coal on a spoil heap. His was the third coal-picking death in the area during the strike. Just over a week later Northumberland miner Fred Taylor was crushed under sandstone slabs while digging for coal on a beach.

Meanwhile, the government tried bribery. In November it offered miners a £650 bonus to return to work. The bribe was accompanied by a press campaign proclaiming that the strike was beaten.

Certain areas were picked out for special treatment by the Coal Board. The most sustained attempt at strikebreaking was made in North Derbyshire. In Shirebrook men who lived outside the close-knit mining community who were known to be hostile to the strike, or who worked a lot of

Coal picking in South Wales. Several miners died and many more were injured trying to scavenge fuel to keep their families warm
Martin Shakeshaft

overtime before the dispute and might be feeling the pinch, were phoned and visited repeatedly, and urged to return to work.

A leader of the National Working Miners' Committee described the operation at Shirebrook: "I've thought things through with management. They suggested we use the phones to call people up – they gave us lists and lent us vans."

Yet as Christmas approached the determination of the mining villages touched the hearts of hundreds of thousands of people. A national appeal led people who had never even identified with a trade union before to give to the miners' Christmas fund. In the mining villages fears of a cold, hungry Christmas evaporated beneath this avalanche of solidarity. The contrast between the courage of the miners and the generosity of their supporters on the one hand, and the inaction of the official leaders of the trade union and labour movement on the other, could barely have been more stark.

Above: Rossington picket, Doncaster, 14 December 1984
John Sturrock / Network Photographers

Right: Children's Christmas party, Frickley, Yorkshire, 7 December 1984
John Sturrock / Network Photographers

Our Christmas will be better than theirs. Of course we will be poorer, but our heads will be held high. And don't worry about our children. They know exactly what's going on. They've been marvellous. They've never moaned when they haven't got 10p to buy a bag of sweets or ice cream.

Rose Tennat, Shirebrook, Derbyshire

Final fights and aftermath

The strikers and their families had held firm against all the odds. By New Year's Day they had stayed out three months longer than their grandparents in the 1926 lockout.

The struggle for a decent Christmas had absorbed the communities and their massive solidarity network. But in the new year both groups had to face up to some hard truths. Peter Walker, the energy secretary, insisted there would be no power cuts that winter, and Peter Heathfield, the miners' general secretary, reluctantly agreed with him.

TUC leaders, who had been promising support in the power stations all autumn, still had not delivered. Despite a resolution backing the miners at September's TUC congress, not a single leaflet or poster had been distributed, not a march had been called.

Worse, when the courts removed the elected representatives of the NUM from control of the union's funds and appointed a Receiver, the TUC – fearful of being found in contempt of court – refused to help. The NUM faced losing its funds, its headquarters, even its phones.

As the legal attacks mounted, the leaders of the power workers' unions relaxed their "guidelines" against using scab coal, oil and gas. Back in the autumn the miners had been assured these would bring power cuts within weeks. But there had been no blackouts.

Once again the Coal Board concentrated its attack on the weaker areas and the weaker pits. The police maintained their presence in the villages, the courts handed down a series of judgements against the NUM and picketing miners, while the media constantly claimed the strike was collapsing.

The last full week of January was a bleak one for the NUM. At Kiveton Park in Yorkshire a group of miners walked to work through the snow. As they returned home after their first day on the wrong side of the picket line, each clutched a plastic sack or shopping bags of coal to warm their freezing homes.

Thatcher and the Tories rejoiced, believing thousands more would rush back to work, but still the strike did not collapse. Once again, the activists in the villages and the support groups rallied. More money, clothes and food were despatched to the mining areas. In the villages, activists sought out and tried to help those who they feared might be driven back to work by deprivation.

At Silverwood in South Yorkshire one picket described the process: "Men who haven't been involved in the strike, who then find themselves in very serious financial difficulty, are too embarrassed to come and ask the union for help. It is those miners the Coal Board hopes to break."

One of the last mass pickets in Yorkshire. Police seal off Cortonwood colliery, the pit which sparked the strike, in a bid to get a single scab into work, 29 January 1985
John Sturrock/Network Photographers

The Yorkshire area's got an injunction saying only six to picket – and they've accepted it. No one think's it's right. But the area has told us that if the funds are sequestrated then there will be no money to pay for lawyers. At this pit we've had 120 arrested on serious charges.

Miner, Yorkshire Main

If the men can't or won't picket because of the injunction then it's up to us women to show them the way. We don't belong to the NUM – there's nothing they can do to us.

Miner's wife, Yorkshire Main

Women picket
Yorkshire Main, 21
February 1985
*John Sturrock /
Network Photographers*

"What we've done is go round and explain to people that, no matter what, if they've got a problem, contact us. It has worked. One man I saw had no gas and has three kids. He'd got gas central heating. Just imagine in this weather – no heating, no hot water, no hot food, and three kids. After I saw him I contacted the branch treasurer, who got on to Sheffield Nalgo [now the Unison union]. Within two days we had his gas back on. Now this same bloke is up at 4.30 picketing with us."

By early February the government was beginning to wonder whether the strike might drag on until the summer. However, some miners' leaders suddenly began to talk of a return to work without a settlement.

For months the miners had been fighting for their industry and the survival of their union. Now sections of their leadership were suggesting a pit by pit fight. It was an illusion – if the union could not win a national strike, a single pit could not win on its own. But after 11 months of blood, sweat and tears, many seized on an alternative option. The more it was talked about, the more men broke ranks and returned to work. In the end, the proposal became a self-fulfilling prophecy.

On Sunday 3 March a miners' delegate conference met. Outside, a desperate lobby of men who had been sacked chanted, "We're not going back." But inside, the delegates voted 98 to 91 – against the will of

Arthur Scargill – to call off the action.

After 51 weeks of struggle the strike ended. In every pit village, relief that it was over, and pride at having stayed out through everything the government, police, Coal Board and media could throw at them, was tinged with dread at what the future held.

This was not a defeat like that of 1926. Then the General Strike had been called off and the miners locked out for six months before returning to work, heads bowed, begging the coal bosses for a job.

In 1985 they went back with bands playing and banners flying. The miners had made history and they knew it.

In the months and years after the return to work politicians, establishment commentators and those trade union leaders who stood by while the miners fought alone came up with a series of justifications for the miners' defeat.

They claimed the strike was doomed from the start, that mass picketing could never beat the police, that workers' solidarity was a thing of the past, that the Tories were invincible, and even that the defeat of the strike signalled an end to class politics.

These claims all flew in the face of the facts. The miners came close to victory several times during the dispute.

At the start of the strike the flying pickets almost shut the whole of the mining industry. They stunned the government, forcing it to use unprecedented numbers

66 of police to prevent Yorkshire miners putting their arguments about pit closures to their fellow union members in Nottinghamshire. Had the Yorkshire and Nottinghamshire NUM leaders been more resolute, Thatcher could have been forced to back down.

As the strike progressed, the Tories tried desperately to avoid fighting on two fronts. They found extra money for left wing Labour-controlled inner city councils, and gave rail workers and other groups inflation-busting pay rises. Every time a second front looked like opening, union leaders grabbed whatever extra the government initially offered rather than stand alongside the miners in their fight.

The Tories panicked when the dockers walked out on strike in the summer, but again the union leaders tried to limit the action, lost the initiative and left the miners isolated. When the Coal Board picked a fight with the pit deputies' union, Thatcher ordered Ian MacGregor to compromise, telling him that "the fate of the government was in his hands".

Even then, if the TUC had delivered the solidarity it promised in September 1984 the outcome of the strike would have been very different.

Those who say the strike was doomed from the start hide the real reason for its failure.

The miners were betrayed by leaders of a trade union movement who feared confrontation with the government and the courts more than they feared mass unemployment.

In the aftermath of the strike the Tories did their utmost to finish off the miners and their union. They encouraged the formation of a scab union, the Union of Democratic Mineworkers, and set out to victimise NUM militants. The UDM was proclaimed the "true voice" of the miners by the government and media.

But although the shadow of hundreds of sackings hung over the pit villages, the government remained wary of the miners. It closed pits by stealth, offering redundancy terms that were unheard of for most manual workers. Resistance continued pit by pit – sometimes coal face by coal face – and the government held off privatising the industry as it intended.

In 1990 the ruling class tried a different tack. The Tories had come under growing pressure from a mass movement against the poll tax – which culminated in a riot in Trafalgar Square. They still feared the miners' strength and the popularity of NUM leaders Arthur Scargill and Peter Heathfield. So they launched a smear campaign through the *Daily Mirror*.

We walk with our heads up. The scabs look at their boots. It wasn't the sort of victory we might have won, but we went through the year with dignity.

Lynne Cheetham, Point of Ayr, North Wales

68 **My beloved son David was a rebel. He loved and cared for his fellow man and the working class of this country. He cared for them so much that he gave his life to the struggle of his union for the basic right to save jobs which should be everyone's birthright.**

Mark Jones

March to commemorate the first anniversary of the death of David Jones on the picket line at Ollerton, Notts. South Kirby, a week after the return to work, 16 March 1985
John Sturrock/ Network Photographers

The *Mirror* was owned by Robert Maxwell, who was busy defrauding his own workers' pension fund. It accused the miners' leaders of accepting money from Libyan leader Colonel Gadaffi during the 1984-85 strike and using it to pay off their mortgages.

It was a crude attack on the integrity of Scargill and Heathfield, and on the memory of the 1984-85 strike. It was also a lie.

Britain's rulers have a long tradition of smearing left wing leaders. But once again the Labour Party and trade union leaders refused to speak out. For six months, helped only by small numbers of socialists and union activists, the miners' leaders battled to clear their names.

It was not until 2002 that Roy Greenslade, the *Mirror* editor who ran the smear, offered an apology. In an article in the *Guardian*, titled "Sorry, Arthur", he admitted that the NUM president was "wronged by the press in general, by the *Daily Mirror* specifically and, since I was then its editor, by me".

When the witch-hunt failed to dislodge the NUM leaders, the Tory government of John Major came back in 1992 with a second pit closure programme, threatening 30 of the remaining pits and 30,000 jobs.

A tidal wave of anger swept Britain. Everything Arthur Scargill had said in 1984 about Tory plans for the mining industry was confirmed. The purpose of the smears against the miners' leaders were also clear. The Tories were determined to destroy the industry.

The whole country rallied to the miners. Trade unionists walked out of work in spontaneous protests. Two enormous demonstrations within a week jammed the centre of London – their size and anger unmatched until the anti-war protests of 2003.

The trade union leaders again promised action to save the mining communities, but once again they failed to deliver. Rather than call a general strike against the Tories, as so many were demanding, they dissipated the anger by calling a series of regional protests which they then failed to build.

This time the betrayal led to the rapid rundown of the mining industry. Fed up with the TUC and offered hefty redundancy payments, miners who had battled through the Great Strike and its bitter aftermath voted to accept closures at pit after pit. The Tories then moved to privatise the few dozen pits that survived.

In some ways this proved a pyrrhic victory. The Tory obsession with destroying the miners reignited the hatred millions of working class people felt for the government, and contributed greatly to New Labour's landslide election victory in 1997.

Twenty years after the Great Strike the mining industry is a shadow of its former self. The union which once dominated the British labour movement has fewer than 10,000 members. But the lessons remain vital for a new generation of activists.

First and foremost, the strike demonstrated the importance of ordinary workers organising and acting for themselves. It was rank and file miners, not their leaders, who launched the 1984-85 strike. It was rank and file miners who took the initiative in pushing the strike forward and then holding it together. And it was rank and file activists in other unions who delivered the solidarity and support that sustained the mining communities for an entire year.

But the strike showed more than that. It demonstrated the power of organised workers to confront governments and big business head-on. Set against the world of Thatcher and her successors – their pursuit of profit over people, their wars, their welfare cuts, their global rape and pillage – it showed another world is possible.

Mirror journalist Paul Foot speaking at a rally to defend Arthur Scargill and Peter Heathfield, Sheffield, August 1990
Steve McTaggart

A chronology of the strike

March

1 National Coal Board announces closure of Cortonwood. Miners at the pit walk out, and call for support from the rest of the Yorkshire coalfield.

5 Strike starts in Yorkshire, with mass meetings in miners' clubs and welfare halls.

6 Scottish and Yorkshire areas of the NUM make strike action official.

8 NUM executive sanctions strikes, but eight right wingers who oppose action call for a ballot.

10 Durham and Kent join strike.

11 South Wales miners vote two to one to stay at work but honour picket lines.

12 Half the country's miners are on strike. Yorkshire miners send flying pickets to Nottinghamshire. Local officials offer to help members scab at Harworth, but most of the afternoon shift stop out. Yorkshire area vice-president Sammy Thompson calls for an end to pickets.

14 The National Reporting Centre, at the request of Nottingham police, drafts 8,000 police officers into the county from half of the 43 forces in Britain. Coal Board brings injunction against Yorkshire NUM, under 1980 Employment Act, to stop flying pickets. It is ignored. Kent miners stopped at Dartford Tunnel. Scottish miners picket Cockenzie power station.

15 David Jones, miner aged 23, killed while picketing in Ollerton, Nottinghamshire.

16 Nottinghamshire vote against strike.

17 Midland North East and North West coalfields vote against strike.

19 Derbyshire area NUM overrules no-strike ballot. Yorkshire NUM found to be in contempt of court, but Coal Board dares not seize NUM assets. NUM members picket 27 Nottinghamshire pits and peacefully persuade their colleagues to join the strike action. Police decide to blockade the county of Nottinghamshire.

22 Power union leaders encourage members to cross picket lines. Train drivers in South Wales sent home after refusing to cross miners' picket lines. 300 miners battle with police and close Haymarket in Edinburgh.

23 Durham miners turn men away at Agecroft colliery in Lancashire.

25 Agecroft vote to strike for a week. Lancashire effectively stopped for the first time.

26 Lancashire NUM joins strike. Scargill tells TUC to keep out of dispute.

27 Picketing at power station stepped up. Eight NUM area leaders urge their members to continue working and again call for a ballot.

28 Yorkshire miners block a section of the M1 motorway.

29 Transport unions impose ban on the movement of coal. It is partially successful. Nurses join the picket lines in South Wales.

April

3 Energy minister Peter Walker calls for ballot. The National Union of Railwaymen (now the RMT) instructs its members to black coal.

5 Nottinghamshire miners vote three to one to remain at work.

10 Emergency debate in the House of Commons on the role of the police in the strike. Two haulage firms take legal action against NUM over picketing of Port Talbot.

11 Pit deputies vote narrowly to strike over closures, but not with the necessary two thirds majority.

19 NUM special conference ratifies strike action in the areas and calls on all miners to rally to the defence of

their industry.

20 Nottinghamshire and Midlands NUM decide to join strike.

23 NUM rules changed so that the required majority for strike action cut from 55 percent to a simple majority. NUM executive member Bill Stubbs hospitalised by police.

24 Arthur Scargill rejects a Coal Board offer to reschedule the pit closure programme.

25 Labour Party National Executive Committee suggests a 50p per member levy for the miners. It is largely uncollected. Yorkshire miners' leader Jack Taylor does deal with the ISTC union to allow 30,000 tons of steel a week to be produced at Scunthorpe works. The original plan was to supply just enough coal to keep the furnaces alight but slash production. The national strike committee orders a clampdown. South Wales leaders pressurise coke workers at Nantgarw to allow 10,000 tons a week into Llanwern steel works (which produces body panels for Ford, BL and Volvo). Miners picket Wivenhoe docks on the east coast.

28 Scargill tells Cardiff rally that there will be no dispensations for steel production at all. Some 90,000 tons of coal are unloaded at Hunterston in Scotland for the Ravenscraig steel works.

May

2 Official figures show more oil being used to counterbalance coal shortage.

3 British Steel use heavy lorries to break through picket lines.

4 Didcot and Aberthaw power stations shut down.

7 1,000 pickets battle with police to stop scab convoy at Ravenscraig works in Scotland.

9 Scottish TUC day of action.

12 Scottish miners' leader Mick McGahey agrees to allow virtually normal steel production at Ravenscraig to protect Scottish industry. 18,000 tons of coal a week are let in – only 6,000 less than normal.

14 40,000 striking miners march in Mansfield, in the heart of the Nottinghamshire coalfield.Police attack as marchers disperse. Those arrested charged with riot.

15 *Sun* workers refuse to print picture of "Führer" Scargill.

16 Anne Scargill arrested with 13 other women. The Women's Support Groups have spread to each area of the strike.

16 & 17: Police attack striking miners' homes in Blidworth, Nottinghamshire. They are looking for 40 Yorkshire pickets.

21 Yorkshire and Humberside day of action. Strike action has been called. TUC general secretary Murray refuses to back it.

22 Hundreds picket Scunthorpe. The Yorkshire leaders' agreement to allow 15,000 tons of coal has been the basis for British Steel to bring in even more.

23 First meeting between union and management ends in no agreement after Coal Board demand pledge of union cooperation in the closing of 'uneconomic pits'. The Aslef and NUR rail union leaders settle for an improved pay offer agreed by the Tories to prevent them striking alongside the miners. The increase amounts to 0.5 percent.

25 Lorry convoys start taking coke from Orgreave to Scunthorpe. High Court rules that miners cannot be instructed to honour picket lines. Scab 'working miner' groups emerge with government and business backing.

30 Scargill arrested at Orgreave and charged with obstruction. More than 80 other miners arrested and 62 injured. This is the second day of an attempted mass picket. Only a few hundred are present after Yorkshire area leaders send pickets elsewhere.

31 Further conflict at Orgreave. Pickets face 3,200 police in riot gear.

June

7 House of Commons debates the miners' strike. Some 10,000 miners lobby parliament. Arthur Scargill says, "I'd dearly love to see every member of the NUM and every trade unionist down at Orgreave." The leaders of the NUM's area unions do not let him organise it. Police attack London train drivers' union representative John Davis. A picket forms at Hungerford rail bridge and escalates to an unofficial stoppage of railway workers at Charing Cross station after management refuse to allow a message of support for the miners to be read over the public address system.

8 & 13: Talks with Coal Board again result in demands on NUM to agree

to management strategy.

12 Welsh TUC day of action. 10,000 march in Cardiff.

15 Joe Green, miner, crushed to death on picket duty at Ferry Bridge power station.

16 Yorkshire Miners' Gala attended by 20,000. Local NUM leaders do not call for mass picket at Orgreave. Ian MacGregor interview in the *Times* marks new government hard line.

18 Second mass picket at Orgreave. 5,000 miners turn up. Systematic police brutality means that for the first time official figures for injured pickets are double those of police. Scargill hospitalised. NUM area leaders back down from building further mass pickets. This marks a crucial turning point in the dispute. Two days later more coke taken out than at any time.

20 Picketing of steel works begins. Llanwern and Ravenscraig starved of coal supplies by rail workers.

27 South east TUC day of action. Rail workers strike for 24 hours. Some 50 schools take unofficial strike action. More than 50,000 people march in support of the miners. Steel union leader Bill Sirs says he will accept scab coal from anywhere.

July

1 Home secretary Leon Brittan endorses use of criminal law rather than civil law against the miners.

2 Strikebreakers take control of Nottinghamshire NUM.

5 Coal Board and NUM hold talks.

6 Coal Board managers start visiting NUM members at home. encouraging them to go back to work.

8 High Court declares NUM annual conference unlawful. National dock strike called against the movement of coal.

9 Dock strike starts. A run on the pound forces highest interest rate so far in the 20th century. The Tories give Liverpool council £8 million in an effort to prevent a fight on a second front. Ongoing talks between union and management show the government is under pressure.

9 Police riot in Fitzwilliam, Yorkshire. Police brutality sparks fightback in several villages. The Coal Board tries to engineer a back to work movement.

10 High Court says NUM conference cannot discuss disciplining strikebreaking members. Scargill ignores ruling.

11 NUM conference passes rule changes in spite of court ruling.

13 North west TUC half-day of action. 20,000 march in Manchester. Government withholds tax rebates to striking miners.

14 25,000 attend Durham Miners' Gala.

16 200 present at resumed picket of Port

Talbot steel works – thanks to dock strike. Local tugboatmen join strike.

18 Nottinghamshire scabs get High Court to make NUM conference decision null and void. More talks collapse. Thatcher makes "enemy within" speech to Tory backbenchers.

19 More negotiations, but after three days no deal is reached.

21 Dock strike ends in shambles after ten days.

31 High Court fines South Wales NUM £50,000 under Tory anti trade union legislation on picketing. It is the first fine on the union under the laws. Labour leader Neil Kinnock says, "The courts will have their way."

August

1 Labour MP Martin Flannery expelled from House of Commons for denouncing tame Tory judges. Kinnock refuses to vote against the expulsion. Chancellor of the Exchequer Nigel Lawson says cost of strike is a "worthwhile investment for the good of the nation".

6 Two strikebreaking Yorkshire miners apply to High Court to force the NUM to ballot on the strike.

10 Special NUM conference rejects Coal Board proposals and increases union disciplinary powers of union against scabs.

11 Women Against Pit Closures

demonstration in London. First meeting of scab National Working Miners' Committee. Nine present.

12 Scabs' committee meets again at the home of Captain Edward Evans of the Christian revivalist 'Moral Rearmament' organisation. Tim Bell from Saatchi and Saatchi is involved, as is David Hart, special adviser to Thatcher. Neil Kinnock, speaking to 60 miners' children from South Wales, condemns pickets' violence.

13 Police refuse to cooperate with the National Council for Civil Liberties investigation into policing of the strike.

15 Scottish strikebreakers sue NUM over ballot.

16 South Wales NUM found in contempt of court for refusing to pay fine in line with TUC Wembley conference policy. £770,000 of their funds seized. NCB warns of large job losses due to deteriorating condition of pits.

20 Picketing stepped up to halt back to work moves at pits. Police violence increases. At Easington, in County

Durham, 1,000 jeer the first scab.

21 Pitched battles between pickets and police at Silverwood colliery in Yorkshire as police take in one strikebreaker.

22 TUC General Council debates miners' strike for first time.

23 Second national dock strike called over unloading of coal by scabs at Hunterston. MacGregor offers working miners 5.2 percent increase if they agree to work overtime.

24 300 shop stewards meet in Glasgow in a conference to support the miners.

29 Thatcher cancels Far East tour because of strike.

September

3 TUC votes to support miners. This support never materialises.

7 NUM leaders agree to tell TUC about forthcoming talks with Coal Board.

9 Talks begin. They last all week, taking place in Edinburgh, Selby, Doncaster and London.

12 Rail workers strike at Manchester Piccadilly after four union members are arrested for collecting for the miners. Agecroft and Bold miners join the picket. Management and police back down.

15 Talks break down. Scargill offers to put dispute before third party. TUC becomes directly involved.

18 Second dock strike ends. British Steel is able to use scab labour to unload as much imported coal as it wants.

24 Vicious police attack on miners and their supporters at Maltby colliery, Yorkshire.

28 Members of Nacods, the pit deputies' union, vote by 82.5 percent majority for strike.

29 *Sun* printers refuse to handle copy which says, "Miners, once the salt of the earth, are now the scum of the earth." Management had refused a union disclaimer. The *Sun* is not printed on the following Monday and Tuesday.

October

1 Arthur Scargill rapturously received at Labour Party conference.

2 NUR/Aslef members sent home for refusing to move coal.

4 Despite NUM lawyers arguing that the case should go to a full trial, the High Court gives NUM five days to

obey the interlocutory injunction and call off the strike.

6 Talks at Acas, the government's conciliation service, begin.

7 Coal Board begins talks with pit deputies.

10 NUM fined £200,000. Scargill fined £1,000 for contempt.

11 Ian MacGregor declares of Acas, 'This place stinks,' and continues to demand NUM concessions.

12 Bomb at Tory conference. Restrictive bail conditions on striking members upheld in the divisional courts.

15 NUM/NCB talks with Acas collapse.

17 Nacods call strike for 25 October.

19 An 84 percent vote against supporting miners by power workers in the EETPU.

21 Michael Eaton replaces MacGregor as NCB spokesman.

24 Nacods leaders unsurprisingly call off strike.

25 Acas prepares formula which both Nacods and NUM accept, and which includes provision for an independent review procedure for proposed pit closures. Courts attempt to seize £200,000 of NUM funds.

26 High Court orders total sequestration of NUM funds.

28 Court moves to make 24 members of the NUM executive liable for the £200,000 contempt fine. *Sunday Times* sensationalises NUM official's visit to Libya.

November

5 Neil Kinnock refuses to speak at a series of rallies with Scargill, saying he is 'too busy'. Blacking of oil won at West Thurrock and Tilbury, and of coal at Didcot power stations.

9 Secret ballot at Bersham colliery, North Wales, sees vote to strike.

1 MacGregor says, 'There is no basis for further talks with the NUM.'

2 NCB offers miners a back to work cash bonus.

4 Sequestrator obtains an injunction from an Irish judge on a Sunday afternoon in his home to freeze NUM funds deposited in Eire.

5 Legal action sought in the High Court to prevent Yorkshire area NUM officers from controlling their funds.

7 NUM resist Sequestrator's application to return union assets to UK, and Dublin Court rules that £2.75 million NUM funds remain frozen and not given to Sequestrator.

10 Transport unions call on international support to mount blockade of coal and oil shipments to the UK.

11 NCB offers £650 Christmas bonus to striking miners who return to work by 19 November.

13 New TUC general secretary Norman Willis condemns miners' violence at South Wales rally.

16 Felixstowe seaman Dave Sanders released after strike in protest at his

Miners march in solidarity with
local council workers in London

John Sturrock / Network Photographers

arrest while on a delegation to mining area.

21 Government increases deduction of supplementary benefits to £16 per week for strikers' families.

23 NCB offer further bribe of £175 to scab by the following Friday.

28 TUC General Council seeks talks with government over miners' strike.

30 After failing to seize NUM assets abroad the courts appoint a Receiver, Herbert Brewer, a Tory Party official from Derbyshire, to control NUM assets and funds.

December

1 South Wales taxi owner killed driving scab to work.

2 Miners' Defence Committee conference meets in London, attended by 1,600 delegates.

3 NUM special conference decides to boycott Receiver.

4 The Receiver, Herbert Brewer, utters the immortal words, "I am the NUM," outside a Luxembourg bank.

5 Ian MacGregor announces plans to privatise pits.

7 TUC says it will not take action in support of NUM for fear of facing contempt charges.

9 Receiver and Sequestrator try to seize £4.6 million of NUM funds from Luxembourg, but again an NUM application successfully

freezes the account.

14 TUC meets energy minister Peter Walker and puts pressure on the NUM to back down.

17 MacGregor dashes TUC peace hopes. Signalman at Coalville in Leicestershire removed from duty by a railway manager for being 'mentally unstable'. He was refusing to handle coal trains.

18 Two drivers at Texaco oil depot in Dagenham suspended for refusing to cross miners' picket line. Strike spreads to Canvey Island refinery.

January 1985

7 NCB claim 1,200 return to work – not the expected surge. Scargill calls for mass pickets at Cynheidre in Wales.

10 NUM executive vote to expel Nottinghamshire area.

17 London Midland and Eastern Region British Rail workers strike in support of three sacked colleagues. Unofficial action on Southern Region shows leaders could have made more of this issue.

February

1 More talks fail to reach agreement.

8 Joint appeal by NUM and Nacods to reopen talks.

11 Solidarity Day. Picket lines all over the country are joined by delegations from most major workplaces.

13 High Court order approves banning mass picketing in Yorkshire pits.

15 Talks collapse.

20 NUM executive rejects deal proposed by TUC.

24 Mass rally in London – many arrests.

28 MacGregor pledges that sacked miners will not be re-employed.

March

2 Yorkshire votes to continue strike.

3 NUM conference votes 98 to 91 to return to work.

Following page: March of the umbrellas – despite torrential rain over a quarter of a million jammed the streets of London in the second mass demonstration in a week to protest at pit closures, October 1992

Andrew Wiard/www.reportphotos.com

Miners joined the 2 million strong march against the war in Iraq on 15 February 2003 – the biggest demonstration Britain has ever seen. The struggle continues…

Above: arbeiterfotografie.com
Right: Jess Hurd/www.reportdigital.co.uk

IN THE CROWD

IMAGES OF
THE JAM
1979 - 1982

Derek D'Souza

visit our website at:
www.marshallcavendish.com/genref

 Marshall Cavendish Editions

The publisher acknowledges the sponsorship by
Delicious Junction towards the publication of this book.

Delicious Junction

www.deliciousjunction.co.uk

1 New Industrial Road, Singapore 536196
genrefsales@sg.marshallcavendish.com
www.marshallcavendish.com/genref

Marshall Cavendish is a trademark of Times Publishing Limited

Other Marshall Cavendish offices:
Marshall Cavendish Corporation. 99 White Plains Road, Tarrytown NY 10591–9001, USA • Marshall Cavendish International (Thailand) Co Ltd. 253 Asoke, 12th Floor, Sukhumvit 21 Road, Klongtoey Nua, Wattana, Bangkok 10110, Thailand • Marshall Cavendish (Malaysia) Sdn Bhd, Times Subang, Lot 46, Subang Hi-Tech Industrial Park, Batu Tiga, 40000 Shah Alam, Selangor Darul Ehsan, Malaysia

978 981 4408 49 3 (paperback trade edition)
978 981 4408 64 6 (hardback limited edition)
978 981 4408 65 3 (DJ hardback edition)

Designed by Jon Abnett at Phoenix Photosetting, Chatham, Kent, United Kingdom

Colour scanning by Tapestry, Soho, London, United Kingdom

Printed and bound in the United Kingdom by Henry Ling, Dorset, United Kingdom

*For Shirley D'Souza: Forever in our hearts,
she will always be loved, remembered and cherished.*

"These pix bring back so many memories. Derek is a nice lad
and it's nice to see these pix in print after all these years!"

Paul Weller
April 2013

Introduction

It was April 1977, a month after my 18th birthday. I had just heard The Jam's debut single, 'In The City', on the radio for the first time. I'd never heard of the band before, but what an intro! A guitar sound that could strip paint at 50 metres, THAT bass line and then THOSE drums! I got on my bike and rode to the nearest record shop to get a copy and find out more. Even though I must have heard it a thousand times since, this song still makes the hairs on the back of my neck stand up, and the lyrics are as relevant and meaningful now as they were back then.

A couple of weeks later, I picked up my copy of the 'In The City' LP on the day of its release (a pattern with Jam releases over the next few years). Bill Smith's sleeve was so striking. I studied it many times, wondering who these guys were and what they were like. They certainly looked 'hard'. Their sound had an edge in keeping with the new wave bands but their look set them apart from most bands at the time. Black suits, white shirts, black ties. While I loved the energy of punk and new wave, the punk 'look' didn't really do it for me. To a schoolboy then, The Jam's stage clothes weren't a million miles from your average school uniform, and were in complete contrast to the punk look. Even the sprayed Jam graffiti logo was so distinctive – I remember drawing it on stickers and sticking them on the back of my schoolbooks. I also remember spraying it on windows when helping with the cleaning at home! (I have a photo to prove it.) It really was "just a thin clean layer of Mister Sheen looking back at me".

The debut LP was so intense and exciting; everything played at 400 miles an hour. I remember seeing The Jam on *Top of the Pops*, full of energy and pent-up aggression with Paul and Bruce jumping in the air. They were certainly exciting to watch and finally, here was a band I could relate to, with members who were of the same age as me.

During the late 70s and 80s I started going to see live bands a lot. I had a little plastic envelope and there would always be at least a couple of tickets in there for upcoming gigs. Considering their immediate impact on me, I can't remember why it took so long, but it was a whole year before I finally got to see The Jam live.

My dad bought me my first 'proper' camera on a family holiday to Guernsey when I was 19, a Petri MF-1. It was a manual camera so I had plenty to learn but I'm sure this gave me a good understanding of the basics.

The following year, I made what seemed the natural step to combine two of my passions – photography and music. I decided to try taking photos at gigs… how hard could it be?

I took my first photos at a live gig at the Rainbow Theatre on 2nd December 1979 – The Jam were a couple of weeks into the *Setting Sons* Tour. My first venture was pretty much a total disaster, with the exception of a couple of shots! Taking photos under stage lighting conditions is one of the most challenging for photographers. In the crowd you're amidst thousands of fans, and everything and everyone is moving. The lights and colours are constantly changing, and the light is rarely bright enough. Half the time it was hard enough to even stay on your feet at gigs, let alone take photographs! It was a case of 'click and hope', and then waiting for your prints to come back and seeing how bad they were.

The results improved with practice, and I learnt to make the best of the equipment I had. In 1981, feeling a little more confident, I sent some photos I had taken at gigs and soundchecks, plus a few I took off the TV (from the 'Start!' video), to The Jam fan club and got a letter back from Paul Weller, saying how much he liked them as they had 'fantastic colour'.

Later, I sent some more photos to the fan club, never imagining the chain of events about to unfold: a missed phone call from Paul's mum Ann and trips to Woking, which eventually led to me being invited by the band to be the photographer for the *Absolute Beginners* single session. The session went well and the band decided to use some of my shots for the rear of the sleeve and the lyric sheet. *Absolute Beginners* went to No. 3 in the UK charts and the rest, as they say, is history!

Fast forward to 1984. I had the idea of putting together my own book of Jam photographs, mostly featuring my own images, but also including the work of two other photographers, Alan Perry and Pete Still, who had photographed the band at gigs between 1977 and 1979. Between us we had 1977–1982 covered. A good friend of mine named Sarah Kent and I designed and mocked up our idea of the book. Of course it had to be named after the title of a Jam song, and that song was 'In The Crowd' – not because of the message in the lyrics but because that was how I had seen the band over several years and how most fans would see them.

We had it all planned – we knew which images were going to feature, the colours, the fonts… everything. I still have the handwritten notebook to this day, and luckily most of it is in Sarah's handwriting, which means it remains legible! Sadly, Sarah was diagnosed with cancer and tragically died in her twenties. After that I had little interest in continuing with the book.

Leap forward to 2012, when I was contacted by Jon Abnett (we had spoken and emailed over a few years but had never met). Jon asked if I would consider allowing some of my photos to be used for the forthcoming Jam book he was working on, *Thick As Thieves – Personal Situations With The Jam*. While I still hoped to have my own book published one day, I didn't see the point of my photos sitting in boxes never seeing the light of day. And as the book was based on many Jam fans' personal experiences with the band, how could I refuse? As a fan I wanted to be part of it, so I immediately agreed.

Stuart Deabill (co-author with Ian Snowball) interviewed me, and captured the story of my involvement with The Woking Wonders. As there were to be so many of my photos in the book, Jon persuaded the publishers to let me have my own chapter, which was a nice touch. Top man!

On 17th June 2012, Jon Abnett and I finally met at the recording of the Zani TV video interviews to promote the book. The book was terrific and has been very successful, and very popular with The Jam's army of fans – amazing when you consider that the band had split up over 30 years ago. It just confirms just how much this band meant to so many and still does to this day. I was naturally excited to have my photos and story in there, but I also wanted to see the other images and read other fans' stories, and their personal experiences with The Jam.

The success of *Thick As Thieves* paved the way for me to create my own book. So much had already been written and said about The Jam that if I was to do a book it had to be different and it had to be now. Jon contacted Chris Newson at Marshall Cavendish (the publisher of *Thick As Thieves*) about producing a book based on photographs, and fortunately, Chris said yes!

For many fans, The Jam was about so much more than the music; it was your clothes, your shoes and your hair. At the gigs, it was the huge feeling of anticipation, that you were not only about to see and hear something amazing, but be and feel a part of it too! The gigs were frenzied affairs – there was always a chance it could ignite a brawl between some rival factions or even rival football supporters. I have never seen this feeling captured on video. How *do* you capture a feeling? Paul had this way of playing that often sounded like there were two guitarists, lead and rhythm at the same time, and Bruce and Rick provided a solid background. And while they were clearly all talented individuals, The Jam as a whole was greater than the sum of its parts.

I don't think I have ever come across a band that had such a close relationship with their fans. I suspect this was very much down to the band, and to Ann and John Weller. At soundchecks, if we got there early enough and there weren't too many of us, John would nearly always let us fans in, and Paul, Bruce and Rick would often (if not always) come out to talk to fans after the gig and sign autographs. I remember turning up with a stack of photos to show the band and they signed the lot! These were just a few of the reasons why there was such a solid bond between the band and their fans, a mutual respect that remains until this day.

The photos I took of The Jam, whether at soundchecks or gigs, are just moments frozen in time. It's difficult to capture the exact feeling, but they can help restore the memory of what it was like being at a Jam gig or being there with other fans at a soundcheck. In this respect they remind me of sports photographs, capturing that single moment forever.

I hope you enjoy the photos; I certainly enjoyed being there and taking them. Even though it was pretty scary sometimes, I would always be hopeful of getting that shot…

In The Crowd is the culmination of a journey that started 33 years ago, and what an amazing journey it has been! Good and bad, scary and sad. "In the city there's a thousand things I want to say to you" – and in this case I truly hope "a picture is worth a thousand words".

Derek D'Souza

February 2013

Derek D'Souza was a name I was familiar with many years before I 'met' him over the phone about 7 years ago. He was well known because of the *Absolute Beginners* back cover shot. A familiar face among the Jam circle had given him my details after I'd worked on Twink's book, *The Jam Unseen*, and once again Derek and I discussed doing a book. It was clear that his passion matched mine when it came to The Jam, so something had to be done!

Over the coming months we spoke a lot on the phone, always promising to meet up and discuss 'a book'. Conversations over email and of course the phone continued. Fast forward to early 2012, when I discussed the idea of using some of his images in a forthcoming book, *Thick As Thieves*. Derek agreed and I put him in touch with Stuart Deabill, one of the co-authors. Due to additional space and the fact that Derek had further ideas for his own book, we agreed for Derek to have his own smaller section.

Around this time I was also working with Universal and Storey Design on *The Gift* (Deluxe Edition). I asked 'Del Boy' if he had anything special that could be used. When he sent me the 'windmill sequence' (see pages 86–87) I was blown away and passed it to Mike at Storey, who used it for the front of the live CD.

It was at the promo film for *Thick As Thieves* that Derek and I finally met, after all those years of communicating through cyberspace and phone calls! We chatted over a few beers and 'the book' was again mentioned…

It was obvious that Derek's images were in demand and at the Pretty Green signing for *Thick As Thieves*, he mentioned that he was going to hold an exhibition of his photographs at Tapestry in London. This turned out to be his highly acclaimed 'Absolute Luck' exhibition. Over the coming months, all the people involved worked incredibly hard but no one harder than Derek, who had to keep up with his day job while sorting out his favourite images to be used, dealing with Tapestry, checking the venue, buying beer and food, etc.

Taps (as they are affectionately known) were very generous but Derek and his wife Krissie dug very deep into their own pockets to supply the food and drinks each night, and even while he was on holiday in Florida, I was emailing PDFs of the catalogue for him to look at.

With the success of *Thick As Thieves* and 'Absolute Luck', I asked Derek if he wanted me to approach Chris Newson of Marshall Cavendish about publishing a book of his images. It did not take long for Chris to say yes.

Again, Tapestry have been very generous, agreeing to take care of all the colour scanning and re-touching. Hopefully, all the hard work from everyone involved with 'Absolute Luck' has paid off, and now with this book, its legacy is there for everyone to see.

With any photographic book the images need to be as large as possible, so it made sense to have one per page. The book's extent was originally slated to be 160 pages, so Derek set about sorting through and finding 160 of his favourites. The idea was that we would then whittle them down, but it soon became apparent that this would be difficult – so they have all been included and the extent of the book increased to 176 pages! Even though this is Derek's own book, he always listened to reason.

He was also keen to include a small section about his exhibition, which includes quotes from some of the attendees – another nice touch from Derek, involving fellow Jam fans. This is not self-indulgent by any means, he simply wanted to say thanks!

Derek's input into this book has been invaluable, it's been great working alongside him and although this book has been years in the making, in reality it has only come together in the space of a few months … and is hopefully worth the wait!

Jon Abnett
February 2013

SETTING SONS TOUR – Rainbow Theatre,
Finsbury Park, London – 2nd December, 1979 (Concert)

When You're Young – Setting Sons Tour 1979

I answered an advert in *Record Mirror* from a fan wanting to swap a ticket for one of the Jam's three nights at The Rainbow for a different night. That guy was Mick 'The Mod' Hughes (we're still friends to this day). We met up at the gig – it was 2nd December 1979 and the first time I had taken my camera to a Jam gig. I'm sure it was the *very* first gig I took photos at! I was wearing the camera body almost like a shoulder holster so it was behind me and would not be noticeable even during a quick search by the doorman. I tucked the lens into the rear waistband of my jeans and had three rolls of film hidden. I wore a M65 army jacket as it was fairly loose, and would hopefully keep the camera equipment hidden.

Security was a breeze and I was in! Our seats were on Bruce's side, towards the right of the stage in Row G, maybe 20 to 30 rows from the stage. When the lights went down I quickly assembled my camera and lens. I was shooting with 400 ASA film (the fastest I could get) and I had set my camera on 800 ASA, fooling it into thinking there was more light than there really was. I happily clicked away using all my film and was hopeful that I had got some good shots even though it was very dark. The gig was the usual frenzied affair and the band looked great (Paul wore the distinctive reflection suit with opposing black and white panels). I couldn't wait to get the film back and see how I had fared.

I sent my films off for developing and when I finally got them back, I wondered if there had been a problem at the lab. Or was there a fault with the camera? Perhaps the films were from a faulty batch? Sadly, none of the above! I took the negatives to the local camera shop – the negatives were almost completely clear and nearly all of the images were blurred, under-exposed (not enough light) or both. The guy shook his head but could not offer any advice on what I should do, THANKS!

These days a quick search on Google is all it would take, but back then it was phone calls to camera shops and a trip to the local library. I found out a bit more about what to do, but the only way to be sure was to try again, and soon! It was pure luck that I managed to get a couple of images out of the 100+ photos I took; grainy but just about acceptable. No matter, it was my first gig, and it was The Jam. OK, the overall results were a resounding failure, but it was a start! (Although I would not know about 'Start!' until the following year.) Things could only get better...

RAINBOW THEATRE 315
FINSBURY PARK

M.C.P. presents
THE JAM

at 8 p.m.

Sunday DEC 2

STALLS

£3.50

G 26

Incl. VAT

TO BE RETAINED   For conditions of sale see over

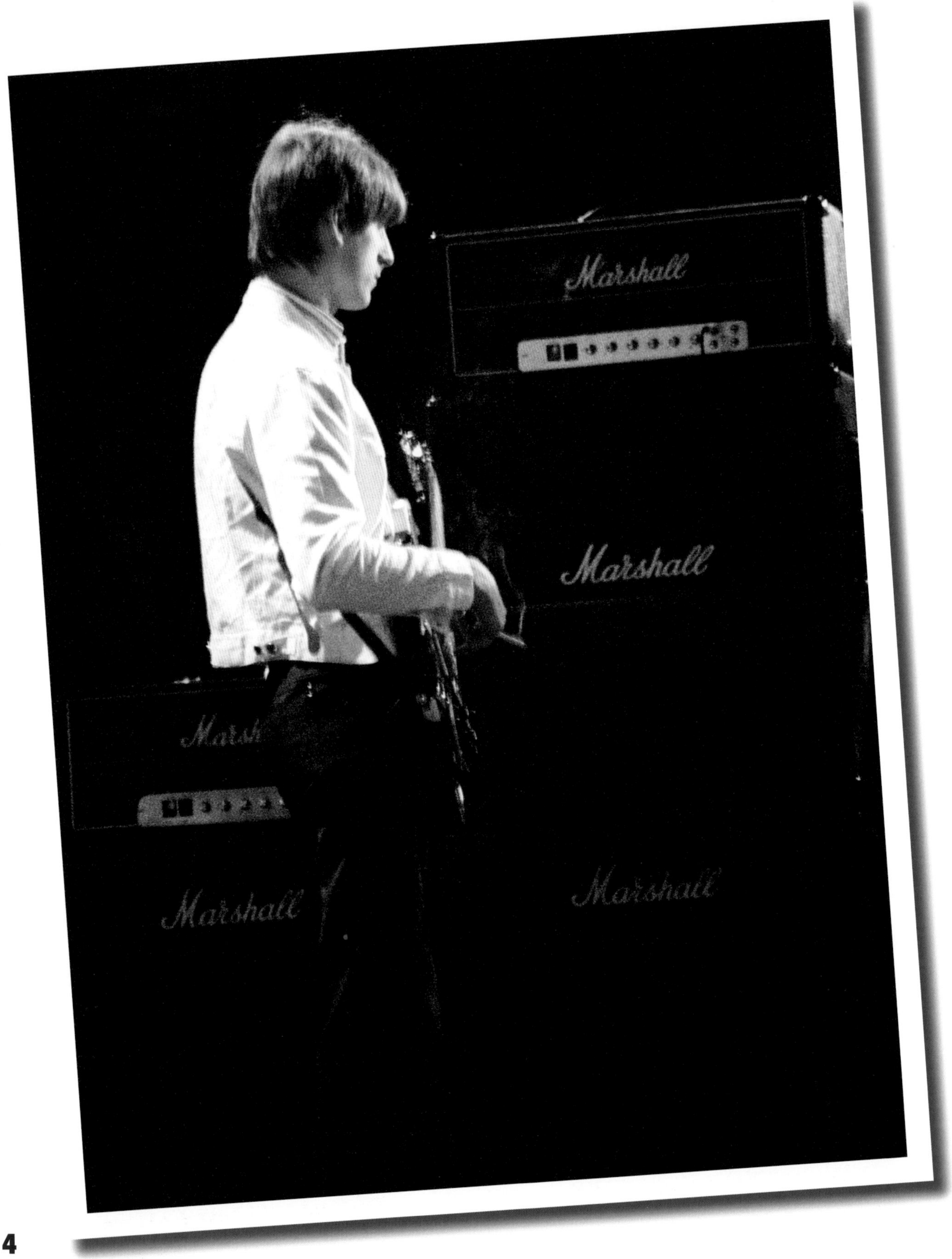

Saturday's Kids

OK, so I wasn't a kid, I was 21! I'd spoken to the band a few times after gigs; they would often come out after the show. They were friendly and keen to talk about their music and very obliging when it came to signing things. On one occasion at the Hammersmith Odeon, I had given Paul my Papermate pen to sign some photos after the gig. After signing a few items, and not sure whose pen it was, he asked, "Is this yours?" Perhaps a little starstruck, I said no. (I didn't remember it was mine!) Paul smiled and said, "I'll have that then," and put it in his pocket! Paul, if you ever used the pen to write a song, please let me know!

SOUND AFFECTS TOUR – Hammersmith Odeon, London – 18th November, 1980 (Soundcheck)

SOUND AFFECTS TOUR – Hammersmith
Odeon, London – 18th November, 1980
(Concert)

ODEON HAMMERSMITH Tel. 01-748-4081
Manager : Philip Leivers

ADVANCE BOOKING TICKET

CONCERT As advised at the time
DATE   of purchase. (See re-
TIME   verse). Please see full
PRICE   seating plan on display

STALLS

BLOCK

21   I   T12

NO TICKET EXCHANGED NOR MONEY REFUNDED
This portion to be retained   No re-admission

25.4.81

Dear Derek,

　　　hopefully you will have recieved you photos back, signed, sorry about the delay.

　　Anyway I just wanted to add that I thought they were great. I especially liked the ones taken off the T.V. fantastic colour!

　　　I'm hoping at some point in time to compile my own JAM book and would very much like to use some of your pix, so if (and when!) the time comes I will obviously let you know and inform you about it oh?

　　　all the best-

　　　Paul Weller

RAINBOW THEATRE 508
FINSBURY PARK

M.P.P. presents
THE JAM
at 8 p.m.

Wednes JUNE 17

STALLS

Incl. VAT £4.00

56

TO BE RETAINED   For conditions of sale see over

**Rainbow Theatre, Finsbury Park, London – 17th June, 1981
(Soundcheck)**

BUCKET AND SPADE TOUR – Guildford Civic Hall – 7th July, 1981 (Soundcheck)

3113
2nd - CHEAP OFF PEAK
NEW MALDEN
FARE
(S)
GUILDFORD
via Cobham
or Woking
AND BACK
For conditions
enquire ticket office
NOT TRANSFERABLE
81

MCP
GUEST
PASS
NAME GUEST +1
ARTISTE JAM
DATE 7:7:81
AUTHORIZED BY
TGP.

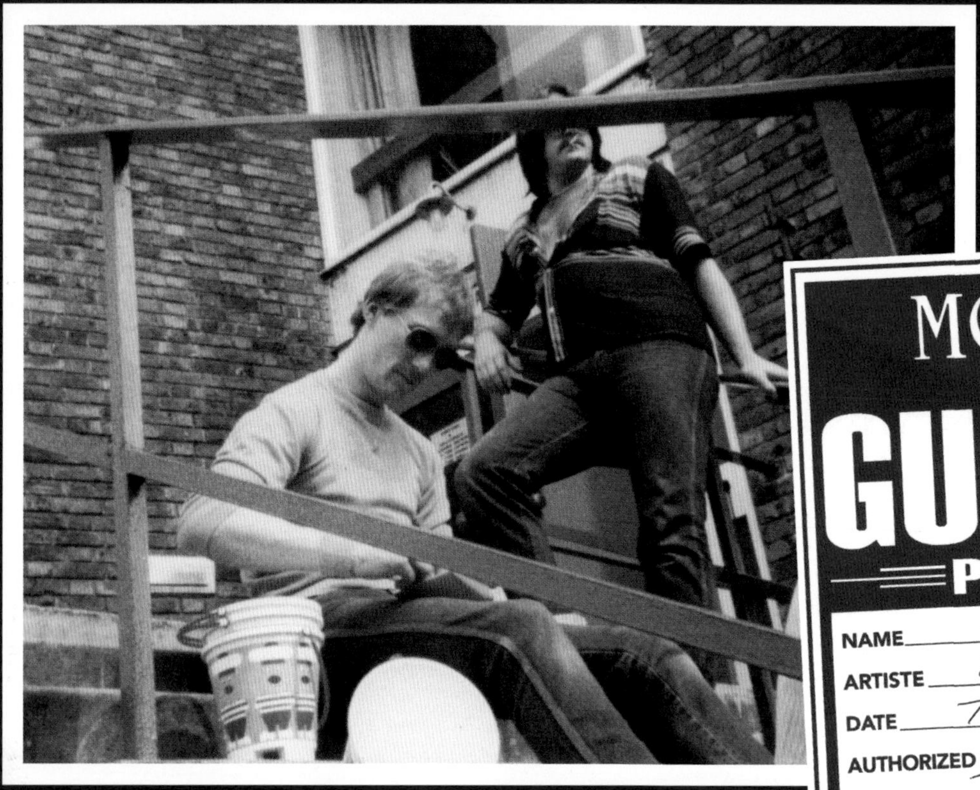

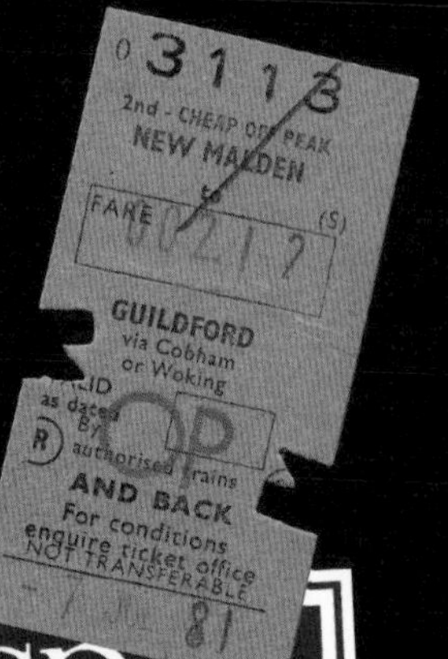

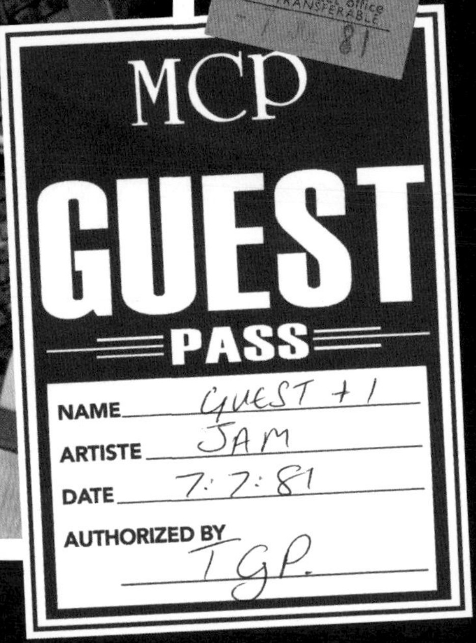

Summer of '81 'Heat Wave' – Four riots and a royal wedding

The summer of 1981 was a hot one! That year, the band played two hometown gigs at the Guildford Civic Hall on 7th and 8th July as part of their Bucket & Spade tour.

I was on my way to the Civic Hall from Guildford station when I bumped into some girls who were also heading there (we were all hoping we would get into the soundcheck – these had become famous among Jam fans as John and the band would often allow us in). I don't recall exactly who was there that day but think it was Suzanne Krasnowska, Melissa Cowell, Sarah Kent and Julie Pritchard. We stopped off at Woolworth's in town and bought some kids' buckets and spades! How could the band fail to be impressed that we were taking the tour so literally? We took these along and the band happily came out and signed them before the soundcheck. I'm not sure what happened to the bucket but the yellow spade survived and is signed by all three members of the band!

Once again, all the fans that turned up were allowed into the soundcheck. At the end Paul was giving out guest passes for that night and people were going crazy to get one – I wasn't really the pushy type, and was standing towards the back of the throng. I had spoken to Paul a couple of weeks earlier after another gig and despite being at the back I felt he made sure I got one. This could just be my imagination, but who cares! I was delighted as I didn't have a ticket for the gig and it was sold out. The gig was fantastic – despite the heat the band were in top form and I managed to get some good photos from up in the balcony.

I was back at the Civic Hall for the soundcheck on day two. This time, I decided to stay overnight at a B&B rather than risk missing the last train home. I was chatting with some other fans at the soundcheck (their names escape me, but if you read this, get in touch!) who were coincidentally staying at the same B&B. So we agreed to have a drink after the gig and head back together.

That night was even hotter than the first. I remember someone announcing the on-stage temperature as being something ridiculous, over 100 degrees or something like that… it was HOT! I had made my way to the front for the gig and Paul had come out for the encore minus his shirt, with two bits of gaffer tape over his nipples and one over a mole. Sadly, the photo opportunity was missed as I had used up all the film in my pocket camera by that point.

I met up with the others after the gig as arranged – I think we went for a drink first and then headed back to the B&B. When I got there, tired from the heat, the gig and the beer, something just didn't seem right. The place seemed different. Stumbling around in the dark, I tripped over a step I hadn't remembered seeing when I checked in during the day. At last, I found my room (mostly by process of elimination)… or so I thought. I opened the door and went in – to the great surprise of the owner and his wife in their bedroom! "What are you doing here?" he cried, "You should be in the OTHER house!"

The moral of the story is, if you own two or more B&Bs, make sure that is clearly marked on the card! And if you are staying at a B&B with more than one address, find out which one is yours! I have never stayed overnight in Guildford since…

Guildford Civic Hall – 7th July, 1981 (Concert)

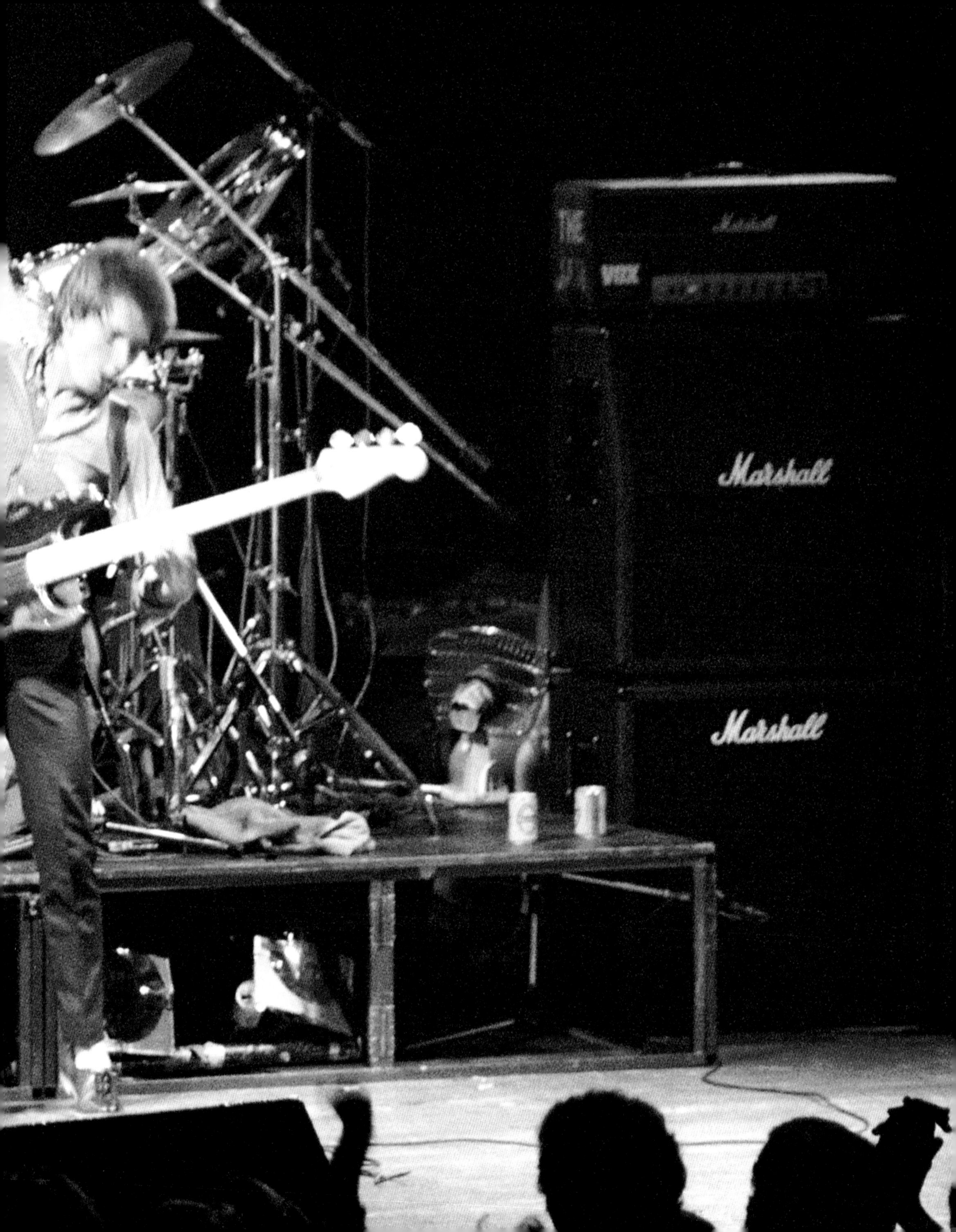

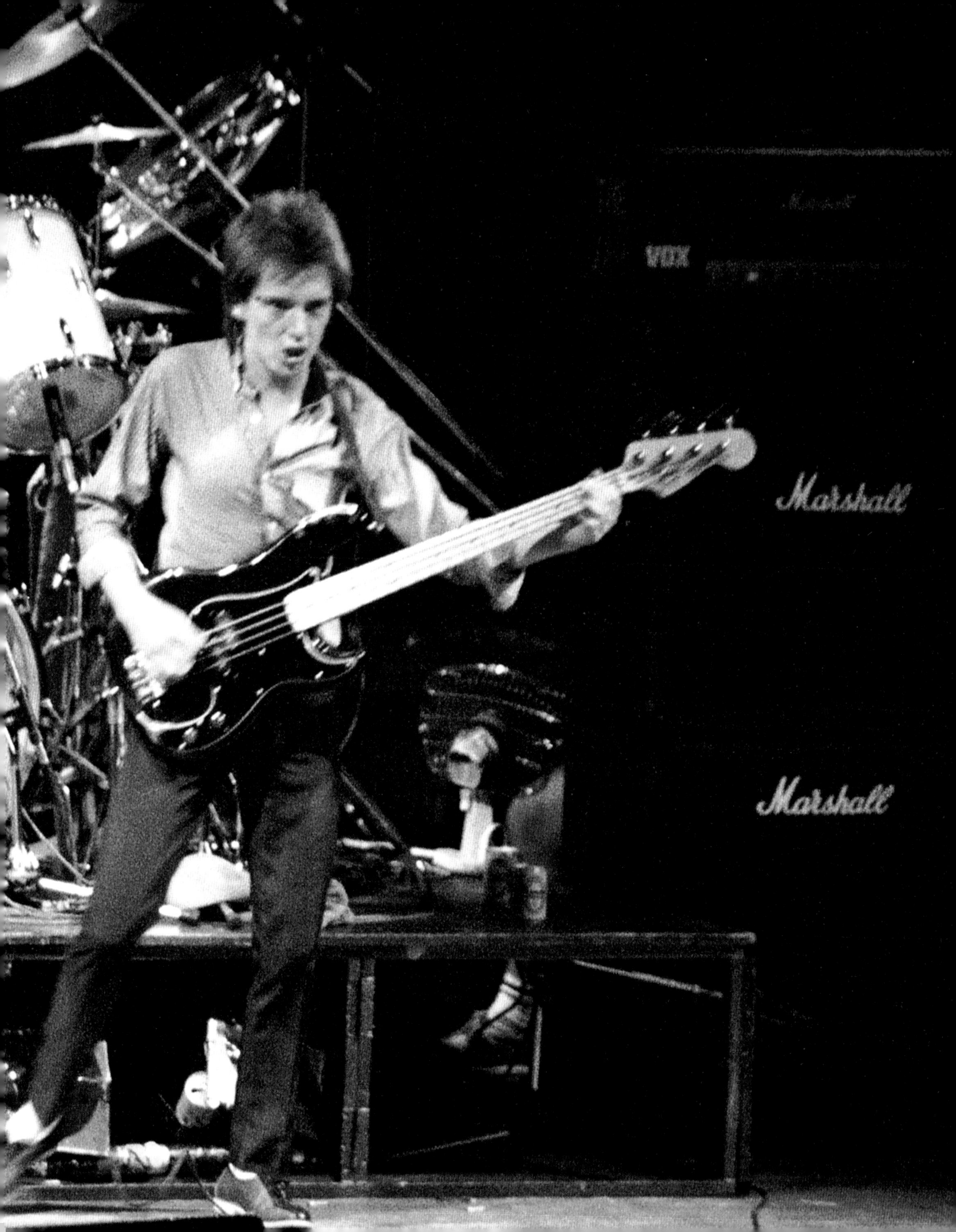
VOX
Marshall
Marshall

1·10·81

SHEERWATER,
WOKING, Sy.

Dear Derek,
Thanks for the photo's!! I
trust that the 'short' pics won't find
there way to the music papers! (joke).
The single sleeve has turned out
pretty good. As soon as we have final
copies I'll forward what you asked for!
It is released on the 16th of this month.
Anyway thanks for all you've done,
Will be in touch,

Bruce.

ROCK   JOHN COLDSTREAM

The Jam

IT TURNED OUT that last night's appearance in Guildford by The Jam was mainly in a good cause—to raise money for a bus which will trundle youngsters to places tranquil or frantic.

In a temperature which might have persuaded a native of the Amazon basin to seize at least twenty winks, the citizens of Guildford divided themselves into two factions to celebrate the return of their fellow county-men.

Upstairs, the stoics sat tight, mouthing Paul Weller's acerbic lyrics with unwavering precision. Downstairs, on the bare boards, it looked like the Kop, with great leaping swatches of half-naked dripping humanity making spasmodic surges across the auditorium.

The cause of this near-suicidal fervour was the unrelenting musical attack by the trio from Woking whose most recent collections of songs boast a title, "Sound Affects," that can hardly fall foul of any trades descriptions' legislation.

Recurring throughout the set last night were all-too-topical references to flames, as in "Funeral Pyre," with dramatic back lighting and "Set the House Ablaze." Weller, dedicated "Man in the Cornershop" to Toxteth!

Always conscious that the best way to get the message across is to pump it loudly and proudly through a first-

rate sound system, the band has never gone overboard on its stage effects: No dry ice, no laser-beams, just the aggressive sparseness available to guitar, base and drums.

By the time the last chords of the signature "It's a Mod World" and "Strange Town" had run through the still night air below Sir Basil Spence's cathedral the crowd was wasted but only slightly thinned: The St John Ambulance lady said a mere three had lost consciousness.

Anna Instone award

A 20-year-old oboe player from Streatham, Julia Girdwood, who won the Shell-London Symphony Orchestra music scholarship in 1977, has won the Anna Instone award for post-graduate music studies. The award, worth £2,500, is made annually by Capital Radio in memory of Anna Instone, who presented the station's classical music programme, The Collection, after retiring from the BBC.

A murder for Moscow

A thriller about the murder of a prostitute in a northern city has been selected as the official British entry for the Moscow Film Festival. Called "Brothers and Sisters," it is a British Film Institute production.

The director of the film, Richard Woolley, will be in Moscow for the screening on July 15.

GUILDFORD CIVIC HALL
OUTLAW PRESENTS
THE JAM
Wednesday 8th July 7.30pm
ALL TICKETS £4.00
Nº 0491

3114
2nd - CHEAP OFF PEAK
NEW MALDEN
to
FARE 002.12
GUILDFORD
via Cobham
or Woking
VALID as dated
AND BACK
For conditions enquire ticket office
NOT TRANSFERABLE
- 8 JUL 81

THE·JAM
DREAMS OF CHILDREN

Absolute Luck Part 1

After the Bucket and Spade tour, I sent some more photos to the fan club (Paul had been kind enough to write back after the ones I sent earlier – he especially liked the ones taken off the TV and the colours – I think they were from the 'Start!' video).

A few days later, I was on my way home from work and popped in to the Grafton snooker club in New Malden to have a beer with my dad. After a while he said, "Oh, I nearly forgot to tell you, Ann Weller phoned for you about doing a photo session for The Jam. Don't worry, she said she'll call you back later." I literally ran home as quickly as I could and waited for the phone call. This was early in the week. I stayed in the next few nights but there was no phone call, and I wondered whether someone was pulling my leg… although I hadn't told anyone about sending the photos!

On Sunday night, the phone rang. It was Paul's mum Ann (who ran the fan club with Paul's younger sister, Nikki), who apologised for not calling sooner. "Sorry I lost your number, you haven't been waiting in have you?" "No, no," I fibbed (sorry Ann!). Ann said, "The band really liked your pictures. John and I would like to meet up with you, see what photos you have, and discuss the possibility of doing a photo session with the band." I was gobsmacked. Imagine your favourite band singer, footballer, whomever… asking YOU to do something for them at the height of their fame, outside of your day job. To be honest, at that time I was still learning about concert photography (I'm STILL learning 30 years on!). I had never done any formal session work and there I was, a complete amateur ('Absolute Beginners' was so apt in so many ways) with amateur equipment, arranging to meet Paul's parents, John and Ann!

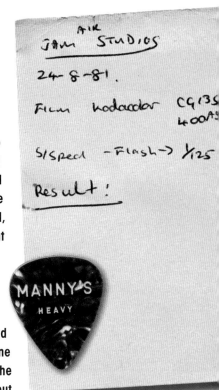

The date was fixed and I packed up some of my best photos and got on the train to Woking. As I didn't drive at the time, Ann picked me up from Woking station. I remember she had a green Fiat X19, which Ann told me she had only just bought. Ann and John were very friendly, setting me at ease straight away. I had broken two fingers on my right hand in an accident a few days before and my hand was strapped up to the elbow. John shook my hand so firmly I was worried he had broken them again! While I don't remember too much of what we talked about, they both treated me well, the way my own parents would treat a visiting friend. No airs or graces, just pleasant hospitality. I don't know if they knew how nervous I was but they were so genuine it certainly helped ease my nerves.

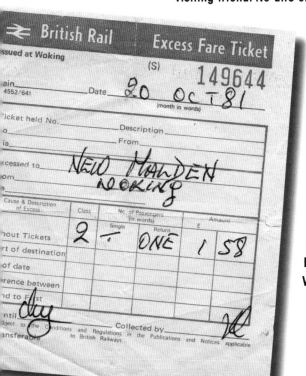

When it was time for me to head home, Ann couldn't work out how to turn on the lights in her new car, so she kindly dropped me at Woking station in John's Mercedes! Each time I returned to Woking, Ann was always helpful and took the time to explain things and give me advice. Even though John and Ann had put me at ease, meeting The Jam was still a major thing for me. I was very excited but nervous, and had no idea what to expect. The appointment was set for 24th August 1981 and I would be meeting the band at George Martin's Air Studios at 214 Oxford Street, overlooking Oxford Circus in the heart of London's West End. The studio was on the fourth floor and The Jam were in Studio 1 (I think). It was handshakes all round as I was introduced to everyone. The band members were all there, along with Dave Liddle (Paul's guitar technician), Pete Wilson (the producer), an engineer that was helping Pete, Kenny Wheeler (The Jam's tour manager), Joe Awome (personal security) and

29

John Robinson (singer/guitarist from the band The Questions). Bruce was recording backing vocals for 'Absolute Beginners' and the atmosphere was quite relaxed, which probably helped my nerves! I remember Bruce trying to match the vocal gymnastics of Paul on the line "Too scared to break the spell, too small to take a fall" (1 minute 37 seconds in on the single!). And after struggling – not helped by him cracking up laughing – I think he left it as is! Paul was working on 'Tales From The Riverbank', another of the band's fantastic B-sides. At one point I was sitting opposite Paul while he was doing the guitar parts. I took a couple of shots, but I was conscious of not wanting to disturb him with the flash as he was working. But I did ask if could have his plectrum and Paul duly obliged. Now if I only knew which one it was! I'm pretty sure it was the Manny's Heavy pick... After a while they decided to take a break. Rick went to play Asteroids (an early arcade game, kids!) and Paul asked if I fancied a game of pool. "Come on, me and you against Kenny and Joe," he said. So there I was in Air Studios with The Jam playing pool, and me and Paul Weller are partners (OK, it was only three frames!). But we won 2–1!

When we sat down to talk about the photo session, Paul already had the location in mind. I don't know why Paul chose Chiswick Park but I will ask him when I see him next, as so many people have asked me that question since! Paul had the idea of wearing dark suits and felt the natural backgrounds would be a good contrast. I didn't know at the time that The Beatles had been photographed there many years ago when making promotional videos (had video been invented yet in 1966?) for 'Rain' and 'Paperback Writer'.

Anyway, we scheduled the session for Monday 31st August 1981. It was my first-ever photo session, for Britain's favourite band (and mine). I didn't really have a clue what I was going to do. I had two camera bodies, Pentax ME Supers, and a couple of budget lenses. I had taken advice and bought four rolls of Kodak Ektachrome 64 slide film (I think Bruce may have told me what to get). The weather was good and I was excited and raring to go!

I had told a handful of fans about the session (not very professional, I know!), and they had all come along. The boys (sorry, I can't remember their names now) hardly said a word the entire time – I think they were pretty overawed by the experience – and after a while they left. The girls, Suzanne Krasnowska and Melissa Cowell, were really chatty and the band responded in kind. The relaxed atmosphere helped me too, and while the band were used to having their pictures taken, this was probably different from most of their sessions. Despite my pre-session nerves, I really enjoyed the shoot. The band was very accommodating and we all contributed ideas. At one point as we walked around the outside of Chiswick House, I noticed the reflection as the band walked past a window. Paul, Bruce and Rick were very patient as I composed the shot, making sure I could see them all in the reflection. This shot was chosen for the lyric insert sheet that accompanied the single.

As Paul had talked about the statues before the shoot, I focused on them too much (no pun intended), but it wasn't easy to compose a picture with a 6-foot man next to a 15-foot statue! On hindsight I would have tried a few lower-angled shots and more close-ups, but the band were looking for a group picture for the record sleeve. I did get some nice ones of the band and some good individual shots, but I would love to be able to do it again... Bruce kept me updated on progress after they had picked the photos they wanted to use – Rick's photo of the rooftops for the front cover, and two of my shots for the rear of the sleeve and for the lyric sheet (a first, I think?). Bruce checked the spelling of my name several times to make sure they'd spelt it correctly, which I really appreciated. 'Absolute Beginners' was released on 24th October 1981 and reached No. 4 in the UK singles chart. The single featured another great Jam B-side, and one of my personal favourites, 'Tales From The Riverbank'. I was proud and thrilled to be involved. It was a nice touch having my name on the lyric sheet with Rick, Bruce, Paul and Bill. I even got a little mention in the October '81 fan club newsletter under the pseudonym of Derek D'Sonza... my big moment spoilt by a typo!

October 81'

Hi,

The Jam's new single will be out on the 16th October 1981 and it is
called Absolute Beginners, with Tales from the River Bank on the
flip side. The photo on the sleeve was taken by Derek D'Sonza who
is a fan club member, we thought we would give him a chance..

AIR STUDIOS – London, 24th August, 1981

ABSOLUTE BEGINNERS PHOTO SESSION –
Chiswick Park, London – 31st August, 1981

31-5-81
J Am - CHISWICK PARK
- 2hrs - 190 pics

4 @ 36 Ektachrome 64
1-4 pics - me super 3 films

mx 1 film (statute & pond
+ pillars all on mx - so
compare.

1 kodacolor @ 135 ASA
100
swap - me super.

Conditions Bright - but
not sunny or hot.
Results.

Tales From The Riverbank

POSP 350

℗ & © 1981 Polydor Records Limited

ABSOLUTE BEGINNERS!
In echoed steps I walked across an empty dream
I looked across this world there was no one to be seen
This empty feeling turned and quietly walked away
I saw no warmth in life – no love was in my eyes.

I stared a century thinking this will never change
As I breathed time rushed onwards without me
You started to break the spell too small to take a fall
But the Absolute luck is – love is in our hearts!

I lost some hours thinking of it
I need the strength to go and get what I want
I lost a lifetime thinking of it
An lost an era daydreaming like I do.

In echoed steps you walk across an empty dream
But look around this world there's a million to be seen
Come see the tyrants panic see their crumbling empires fall
Then tell em we don't fight for fools – 'cos love is in our hearts!

I lost some hours thinking of it
I need the strength to go and get what I want
I lost a lifetime thinking of it
And lost an era daydreaming like I do.

You can lose some hours thinking of it
You need the strength to go and get what you want
You can lose a lifetime thinking of it
And lose an era daydreaming like I do.

The following are all Absolute Beginners
Derek D'Souza – Group Photos
Rick – Front Photo
Bruce – Sleeve Layout
Paul – Art Direction
Cheers Bill!

(Lyrics reproduced by kind Permission of Chappell & Co. Ltd.)

Produced by Pete Wilson & The Jam

THE POETRY OLYMPICS – The Young Vic Theatre, London – 30th November, 1981

That's Entertainment:

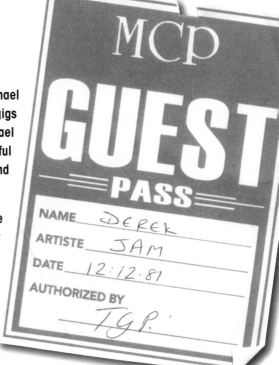

I n the winter of 1981, The Jam played four nights in London – two at The Michael Sobell Sports Centre and two at the Hammersmith Palais. These were the first gigs since 'Absolute Beginners' had been released. I remember arriving at the Michael Sobell Sports Centre in Finsbury Park for the soundcheck (despite the dreadful snow!). A few of the people I had met before at gigs got down on their knees and bowed – they were royally taking the mickey out of me, but all in good fun.

Although it was cold and pretty dark in the venue, we soon forgot about the temperature after being treated to new material from *The Gift*, the band's next studio LP. While the sense of anticipation when waiting for The Jam to come on stage at a gig was always pretty intense, hearing new material gave a different kind of excitement, similar to listening to a new LP or single on the record player for the first time, while you read the sleeve notes or follow the lyrics.

Standouts I recall from the session were 'Ghosts', 'Carnation' and 'Happy Together'. I also remember Paul and Bruce playing 'That's Entertainment' – which I had never heard live before – on their Ovation acoustic guitars… brilliant! The addition of the brass section of Keith Thomas and Steve Nicholl lent a new and different dimension to the traditional Jam sound and our appetites were truly whetted for the new LP, which would be out the next year. That night at the first Sobell gig, the band members were all wearing Lonsdale sweatshirts under their suit jackets (I believe they had just signed a sponsorship deal), and coincidentally, I happened to be wearing a dark blue Lonsdale sweatshirt as well. I was well chuffed! Of course the audience were decked out in Lonsdale T-shirts and sweatshirts the following night, and if I recall correctly, Weller was wearing Fred Perry. It was amazing how so many people would try and imitate the Paul Weller look. I remember going to my local hairdresser Vincent Diplacido with front, back and side photos of Paul from a magazine (it was his early Marriott look) and saying "make me look like that", and him just shaking his head. Oh well, nothing ventured…! The band opened the gig with another of my favourites, 'The Gift' – I loved the Hammond Organ opening on the track. Paul jumped up onto the monitor and nearly fell over, but somehow managed to stay on his feet! I remember getting a photo when it happened, but it wasn't great and to be fair I was quite far from the stage at the time.

The next three nights were equally spectacular and I especially liked Hammersmith Palais as a venue. The hall was fairly wide, but the upstairs section wasn't too far back, so I could get into one of the little booths at the front of the balcony with a good view of the stage. There was less likelihood of being knocked about up there, which made a huge difference when it came to taking photos. One of the highlights for me was the final night when the band played 'Boy About Town'. They had played it the previous night and both Paul and Bruce had jumped in the air at the same time, but unfortunately I had missed the shot. When they played the song again that night, I was ready. I had the whole stage in view and enough frames left on the film, and as the song built up to a crescendo about a minute in, they did it again! I had to wait a few days to get the slides back to be sure I got the shot, but yes I had (see page 108–109). I also loved the fact that John Weller can be seen to the left of the stage – I had never seen John in a photo like this with everyone in view.

This is one of the reasons I love to take photographs at gigs. People have often asked me how I can enjoy watching the gig through the camera viewfinder, but it is the excitement of wondering if you got the shot and then waiting to find out. Of course with digital now you can check the photos almost immediately, but back then I had to wait! Unfortunately, with the equipment I had and the limited access I had at gigs, many photos would be blurred or just too dark. I sometimes wonder how I managed to get anything at all!

XMAS GIGS LONDON – Michael Sobell Sports Centre –
12th December, 1981 (Soundcheck)

XMAS GIGS LONDON – Michael Sobell Sports Centre – 12th December, 1981 (Concert)

XMAS GIGS LONDON – Hammersmith Palais –
14th December, 1981 (Soundcheck)

XMAS GIGS LONDON – Hammersmith Palais –
14th December, 1981 (Concert)

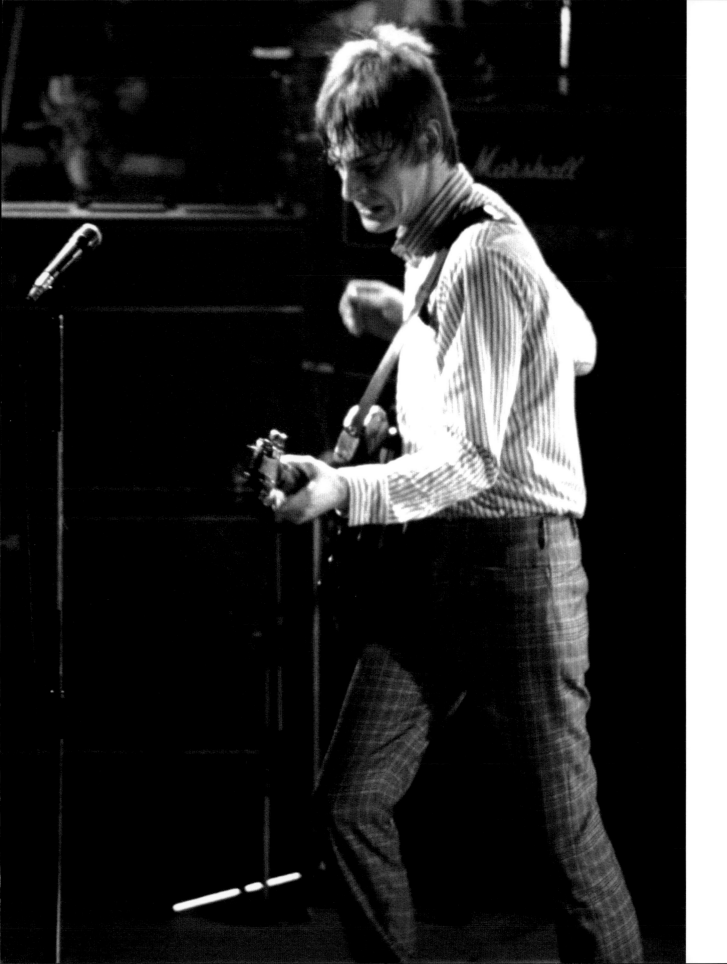

MOVE, MOVE, WE GOT
GO SHOUT IT FROM YOUR
GIVE IT TO ME ONCE,

THE GIFT OF LIFE...
ROOF MOUNTAIN TOP!
GIVE IT TO ME TWICE

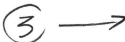

XMAS GIGS LONDON – Hammersmith Palais –
15th December, 1981 (Concert)

Paul Weller (signature)

MJM RECORDS LTD

52 EDEN STREET, KINGSTON, SURREY. PHONE 01-549 1127

111 HIGH STREET, NEW MALDEN, SURREY. PHONE 01-949 4690

54 THE BROADWAY, TOLWORTH, SURREY. PHONE 01-390 3313

30 VICTORIA ROAD, SURBITON, SURREY. PHONE 01-390 3106

148 CENTRAL ROAD, WORCESTER PARK, SURREY. PHONE 337-6007

58 HIGH STREET, DORKING, SURREY. PHONE DORKING 3578

TOGETHER
WE CAN STOP
THE BOMB
24 OCTOBER

Date 23 Feb 1982 Region 15
Category Lit.Sub: No
Includes Lit.Sub: No
Payment by Cash
Date of Expiry FEB 83
Membership Number 132765
DEREK D SOUZA

NEW MALDEN

SURREY

CND
MEMBER

CAMPAIGN FOR NUCLEAR DISARMAM
11 GOODWIN STREET LONDON N4 · TELEPHONE 01 263

The Gift

After much anticipation, *The Gift* was released on 12th March 1982. The new LP was a soulful affair with the new brass section of Keith Thomas and Steve Nicholl, although we had no idea that this would turn out to be the band's final studio album (I still have a copy wrapped in the original paper bag)!

I was off to see the band play five consecutive nights, starting with the Guildhall Portsmouth that night, followed by two nights at the Brighton Centre, one night at The Fair Deal in Brixton, and then The Alexandra Palace in London.

After the gig in Brighton on 13th March 1982, we decided to go to a bar as we were staying over at a B&B. It was my friend Suzanne's 18th birthday, so a few beers seemed a good idea. There were four of us – Suzanne, Peter Deering, Tony Porter and myself. On the wall outside the bar was a backlit neon sign in Day-Glo yellow, about the size of a 42" Plasma TV, that said "Over 21s only" for all to see.

As our turn came to enter, I was first up. "How old are you?" asked the doorman. "23," I replied. "In you go," he said. This was repeated with Suzanne and Peter, until he got to Tony, who confidently replied, "19." The doorman asked him again, and Tony repeated himself with even more confidence. The doorman pointed to the sign, but luckily it was a quiet night and he let us ALL in!

The following morning, one of us spotted the poster for the tour, which featured the photograph I had taken in Chiswick Park the previous year. I was thrilled, and despite being tired from the past two nights' gigs, little sleep and no sign of the day's first coffee, I of course leapt at the chance to have my photo taken in front of it. I never did manage to get one of those posters though. If anyone has a spare…

Tales From The Riverbank

Despite having seen The Jam seven times in March '82, I was desperate to see them abroad. While I had been unable to go for the infamous French gig, the band would be playing at the Paridiso club in Amsterdam. I had visited Amsterdam twice, and been to the Paradiso club once to see British R&B band The Inmates (whom we had seen several times back home) – purely by luck, when we spotted the advertisement at the hotel where we were staying. It had previously been a church until the mid-60s and was an excellent and unusual venue for a gig.

Back to 1982! My good friend Peter Deering and I booked tickets for the Paradiso gig and travelled by ferry from Harwich to the Hook of Holland, and then by train to Amsterdam. After checking into our hotel, we headed over to the club and saw a few faces we recognised. It seemed like the majority of people were from the UK. While the band had not yet started their afternoon soundcheck, there were at least 300 fans milling about the entrance, and security were not letting anyone in at this time.

Luckily for us, one of the band's personal security guys, Chris Adoja, remembered me from before and ushered me in, saying, "You'd better come in, the other photographer's already in there." (Twink was the band's official photographer at the time.) Even though I wasn't there in any official capacity I gladly accepted and Pete and I walked in. There was just the crew and a few people in the hall. We said hello to John Weller and shortly after, the band started their soundcheck. We were very lucky! I got some good pictures but didn't want to overdo it as I wasn't actually supposed to be there.

I decided to leave my camera at the hotel for the actual gig as I had no photo pass. Instead of getting some shots I got a couple of plectrums and a whack in the face! No clue from whom, but luckily, some helpful Dutch guy hauled me back on my feet and despite seeing stars for a few moments, it was on with the gig! The sound at the Paradiso was excellent and the band was in top form.

It was great seeing the band play abroad – a bit like seeing your favourite team win away in Europe after having played a blinder!

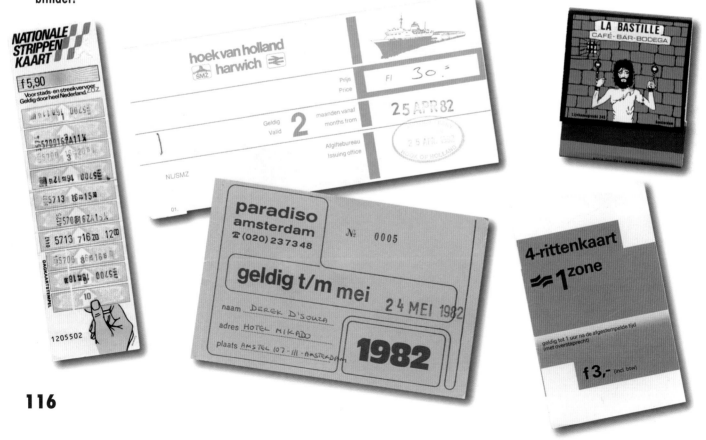

Set The House Ablaze

I t was the very first night Channel 4 was launched in November 1982 and The Jam would be playing live. A few mates and I headed to The Magpie and Stump in Chelsea to watch the band on TV. The show was great and afterwards I stayed for a couple more beers and a frame or two of pool before jumping on a bus to Clapham Junction to get the train home.

On the train were a group of four lads who had seen The Jam on TV earlier and were pretty much slating the band. After two or three stops I couldn't take it any longer and walked over to tell them they were completely wrong and enlighten them as best I could! The conversation did get a little heated, but like Magnus Magnusson I had started and so was going to finish, and I went two stops past my station and had to get a cab home. To be honest it could have been worse, not exactly 'down in the tube station at midnight', but certainly close enough! While my response was not particularly sensible, it says something about the effect The Jam had on my life. They were my band and I was fiercely loyal towards them.

The Bitterest Pill

T he split was announced to great shock all around. I remember bumping into Bruce on London's Kings Road and he was gutted. It was hard to know what to think or to say. Like many fans I wanted them to carry on, but the more I thought about it, the more I believed Paul's decision to stop was the right one, and ensure that the band's legacy would remain intact. The Jam had stood for so much to so many of us fans that if any member of the band were to carry on against their wishes it wouldn't be the same, or worse still, if they carried on and made records of a lesser standard.

I managed to get tickets to eight dates on The Jam's last tour. Thanks again to Ann Weller for helping secure the best tickets, including first and second rows at Wembley (I still regret missing one night out of the five at Wembley to go to a party!). I have read some negative feedback about the gigs, but I felt they were a great chance to say our goodbyes and likewise for the band to thank the fans for their support. I personally felt Guildford should have been the last gig; the closest one to their hometown. I don't know the details of why the Brighton gig was added. I read it was one of Paul's favourite venues, and there was still a huge demand to see the band one last time, plus there was always the Mod association with the town. There was just one small problem – I didn't have a ticket and the clock was ticking!

FAREWELL TOUR – Wembley Arena, London –
1st December, 1982 (Concert)

FAREWELL TOUR – Wembley Arena, London –
2nd December, 1982 (Concert)

FAREWELL TOUR – Guildford Civic Hall – 9th December, 1982 (Concert)

In The Crowd

Brighton, THE LAST NIGHT, 11th December '82 – The additional final gig after Guildford. There were no tickets and no way of getting one. No one was selling and I was worried I had missed the boat. After all the band had meant to me I did not want to miss the last gig; tonight I was a fan and photography was the last thing on my mind.

Security was tight at the Brighton Centre. We didn't see anyone we knew and there were no tickets to be bought but we were determined not to be defeated.

I was with two good friends, Peter and Tony. We went round the back of the Brighton Centre, where there were about 15 to 20 others in the same boat. We considered our options – there weren't many! All of us somehow managed to climb into the back of the venue, without a clue as to where we were in the darkness. The closest I would ever get to an SAS mission!

Eventually we came to a door, and when we opened it an inch or two we soon realised we were backstage as we could see guitars and flight cases. We calmed ourselves and formulated a plan – when the lights went down in between songs, five at a time would take advantage of the darkness and run through the backstage area and over the barrier to be lost 'in the crowd'. It was like the scene from *The Great Escape* when they escape into the woods… but without the woods!

I think I was in the second or third group to go (we were getting edgy, surely we would be discovered soon), when suddenly the lights came up and there we were, like rabbits caught in the headlights. To make matters worse, we had been spotted and Kenny Wheeler was bearing down on us. So I just ran for it and did a 'Superman' dive over the barrier and into the crowd. Quick check – nothing broken, I was in! I'd missed a few songs, but I was in.

To be honest the gig was a bit of an anti-climax. A few idiots chucking bottles, and a mixture of anger, frustration and disbelief all round. At the end, there were people walking around dazed and stunned, many were in tears. I was just glad I had been fortunate to see them as often as I had and that I had the opportunity to become involved for a brief time in my own small way. For five years I had lived my life based around Jam tours – always planning to see the next gig, and looking forward to the next single or album. Even now when I think back to 1978–1982, those years were defined by the Jam LP of each year and the subsequent tour.

It had been an amazing time. I was 18 when it started and 23 when it ended. I didn't really have any regrets, but I would have liked to have seen them more often and earlier on in their career in some of the smaller venues. I also wish I had been more pushy to try and get decent access so I could have taken better photographs and more often. Other than that, I was privileged to see the best band I have ever seen live many times and to have met so many fellow fans. I was proud to be a member of The Jam army, and like so many fans, The Jam was my band and I was fiercely proud of them.

Absolute Luck Part 2

I'm not exactly sure how the idea for the 'Absolute Luck' exhibition came about. I had seen an exhibition of wildlife photographs at Tapestry in Soho a few years before that, and thought it would be amazing to hold an exhibition one day – without my Jam photos in mind. The title was a mixture of 'Absolute Beginners' as I had been involved with the sleeve, and Luck as it was pure luck on my part, and of course the line "and the 'absolute luck' is love is in our hearts".

Time to introduce Alan Patterson, a friend and work colleague, and fellow Jam fan. I had mentioned the *Thick As Thieves* book to Alan, as well as my dream of one day holding an exhibition of some of my photos of The Jam.

In the summer of 2012, Alan contacted Tapestry Group, a design agency in the heart of London's Soho whom we had both worked with in the past. Tapestry's location and history of hosting gallery nights for photographers made them the perfect venue to showcase the event (we also learnt that several of the staff were Jam fans!).

The discussion with Tapestry's Tony Garrett (Operations Director) and Craig Ralph (Client Services Director) was very positive. They liked the images and the story behind them, and I was very impressed by their professionalism. Handing over my prized and irreplaceable collection of slides and negatives was a daunting prospect, but I had total faith that they would be safe with Tapestry.

After the meeting we went to Giraffe Bar & Grill across the road from Tapestry, and as the drinks arrived 'When You're Young' by The Jam played over the sound system. It was not one of the better-known Jam songs such as 'A Town Called Malice', 'Start!' or 'Going Underground', but to me it was a sign!

It had been 30 years since The Jam split up and with many other Jam-related projects going on in 2012, it seemed the right time to exhibit my photos. *Thick As Thieves – Personal Situations with The Jam* was of course a big inspiration; as a result of that book and my small involvement I got to meet many Jam fans and forged some great friendships as a result.

On the final day of filming the documentary for *Thick As Thieves – Personal Situations with The Jam*, I was due to be interviewed by Stuart Deabill about my involvement with the band. (If you haven't read the book, get yourself a copy – it's a brilliant collection of many people's experiences and memories of The Jam.) I finally met Jon Abnett ('Mr. Jam' to many of you) that day, and it was like meeting an old friend. We had spoken on the phone and emailed each other for a few years, but this was the first time we had met face to face.

As Alan and I talked about 'Absolute Luck' with friends and Jam fans, word got around and what originally started as a one-night event grew into a three-week exhibition, with five additional nights in November and December 2012. The gallery was open during the day, but the five private night events were by-invitation only; not to make it exclusive but just so we could manage the whole thing!

None of us had worked on anything like this before so it certainly wasn't easy, and we flew by the seat of our pants on more than one occasion. To make matters worse, I was on holiday in Florida for two weeks before the exhibition started and as such had to do quite a bit from afar, but fortunately, I had the A-team working on things at home.

In the end over 600 people attended the exhibition, which was amazing! Everyone seemed to enjoy recalling and sharing times that meant so much to so many, confirming that the band that had been such a big part of our lives was still held in the highest regard to this day.

I have great memories of the event. Personal highlights include:

- Walking up and seeing the window for the first time on opening night (while getting a parking ticket!);
- Transporting several hundred bottles of beer, two packets of crisps and a packet of salted peanuts (for Colin!) in our poor car!
- Meeting old friends and making many new ones, sharing stories with fellow fans, signing copies of the catalogue for the ladies from my team at work, and them raising a glass to me over dinner (god bless ya girls!);
- Andy McDonald who drove all the way from Scotland for opening night (sadly he couldn't even have a beer);
- Tony Fletcher who popped in from New York;
- Tony Egan for his words of support and encouragement when I needed them most;
- My dad being there to witness the event on the night we had so many good friends and my extended family visit, but also being gutted inside that my dear mum, who sadly passed away, could not be there to see it;
- Pete Steadman, Ron Ball and Jess' dad – three massive Jam fans who each won one of the limited edition prints we raffled;
- Paul Dimmock, who hasn't given up hope that he still holds a winning raffle ticket – and reminds me of this every time we speak!
- Vic Falsetta (and that shirt) for kindly accompanying Ann Weller on the last night. I contacted Ann at fairly short notice and hadn't seen or talked to her in quite a few years, so I was genuinely nervous to see her after so long. I needn't have worried as Ann was her usual self, and it really was the icing on the cake for me that she took the trouble to attend. It was a shame my dad came on a different night; I would have liked them to meet each other.

We had a great mixture of people from the press and music business, corporate guests, work colleagues, family, friends and fans of The Jam. Some came back more than once and we even had a few gatecrashers!

It's impossible to express just how much this meant to me. To quote Paul Weller, "What have I learnt? BELIEF IS ALL!"

Thanks to you ALL!

x

Derek

Absolute Luck

Photographs of the The Jam
by Derek D'Souza

A fascinating exhibition of Derek D'Souza's photographs of the greatest band of all time, The Jam. The venue was an atmospheric and intimate Soho gallery, but it didn't steal the show from Derek's astounding images. As a lifelong Jam fan, I have seen endless images of the band over the last 35 years and this series of vibrant pictures has managed to capture the band at their best with rare, usually unseen, relaxed moments.

Gina Guarnieri

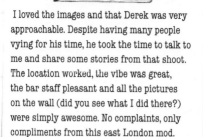

I loved the images and that Derek was very approachable. Despite having many people vying for his time, he took the time to talk to me and share some stories from that shoot. The location worked, the vibe was great, the bar staff pleasant and all the pictures on the wall (did you see what I did there?) were simply awesome. No complaints, only compliments from this east London mod.

Paul McKenzie

A fantastic evening in a wonderful venue. Derek's photography captured perfectly what I remember as the excitement and youthful energy of The Jam in concert. The Chiswick photos show the band at their sartorial zenith with Weller effortlessly pulling off the Small Faces' Steve Marriott. Derek's photographs and the evening as a whole made a bloke of almost 50 feel 15 again, and for that, I thank Paul, Rick and Bruce and yourselves!

Martin Gainsford

A great exhibition, great photographs. Nice to see that in this modern age when everything is so visual, that pictures taken 30 years ago still show out in quality. This is even more special when you consider it was a fan rather than a pro who took the pictures, and at a time when there were none of the advantages of modern sensitive cameras, and not having the capability of seeing the images right away, having to wait instead to have the films processed and seeing the results.

David Coombs

Brilliant exhibition that took me back to those good old days. Great images that captured the moment and kept the memories alive. Thanks to Derek and all involved. Superb!

Pete Steadman

Excellent exhibition, lovingly presented at Tapestry in a nice setting.

Mark Baxter

Fantastic exhibition, great photos, superb atmosphere and venue. Very professional.

Colin Foster

Walking into Derek's photo exhibition was like walking into the photo shoot at Chiswick Park. The enlarged images filled the room with the presence of The Jam. Those eerie and atmospheric photographs have always been my fondest of the band. It was a special occasion and I'm glad that I didn't miss it. The images, the exhibition and the people at the event celebrated one of our favourite bands and helped to share what must have been an incredible day out for Derek, who is no longer an Absolute Beginner.

Ian Snowball

At the exhibition I was taken aback by the love and effort taken into finally getting Derek's photos out into a public place, and to be part of 2012's celebration of The Woking Wonders. Derek's pictures are as iconic as any I've seen of The Jam, and the fact they were taken not from the Press Pit makes them even more precious to The Jam Army, as he was one of us.

Stuart Deabill

Derek's images capture an unforgettable moment in time – for those fortunate enough to experience The Jam first hand and for those who would willingly swap a piece of their youth to have been part of it. The fact that Derek was afforded the opportunity to, as a fan, take these photographs is testament to how in touch the band were. They represent an era in British music that is just as relevant and influential as the 60s only less publicised. Tapestry was an ideal venue to exhibit Derek's stunning work. I loved it. Well done to all of those involved!

Elise Bowes

I really enjoyed the exhibition, especially the changing photos on the video screen. All the photos looked great.

Lisa Pevovar

I really enjoyed the exhibition; the venue was great. I walked away having bought two prints, so I guess I really liked it! Would certainly attend a similar event, and will definitely buy more of Derek's work.

Stephen Moon

I thought the whole night was absolutely superb. It was brilliantly organised and hosted and the photos were amazing. I was thoroughly bowled over by the whole event. I can't thank you enough for putting on an exhibition like this and allowing fans to come.

Thomas Kehoe

Gr8 Photos, Gr8 Vibe @ The Exhibition, Gr8 2 Meet Derek, Hope it was a Gr8 Success 4 Him. Gr8 Memories From Days Long Gone!

Dean Powell

'Absolute Luck' was a terrific exhibition. I was a loyal Jam fan and vividly remember Derek's pictures of the band. What I didn't know was the backstory. It's another example of why I loved The Jam – the gigs were the best, but unlike most other bands, they genuinely cared about their fans. Giving Derek a break says a lot about the band and John and Ann Weller.
The photographs captured The Jam's style, energy and the excitement of the gigs. I was 14 when I saw four out of the five nights at Wembley and the images from that night brought back great memories of my formative years.

Ed Mylles

From the moment this was advertised, I could not wait to attend the exhibition. I am amazed that after more than 30 years, The Jam still means so much to so many people. The crowning glory for me was winning a limited edition print – I chose the one from the Guildford gig on the farewell tour, and I still say that should have been the last night!

Ron Ball

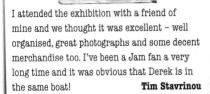

I attended the exhibition with a friend of mine and we thought it was excellent – well organised, great photographs and some decent merchandise too. I've been a Jam fan a very long time and it was obvious that Derek is in the same boat!
Tim Stavrinou

A fantastic evening. It was a true privilege to view so many of Derek's iconic photographs of The Jam and to meet Derek in person, an absolute professional who shows such enthusiasm and passion for his work.
Mike Storey

I really enjoyed the evening. It was great to bring my wife and relive those times with her. Great images!
Dave Noonan

The exhibition was bang on! Free drink, looking at brilliant never-seen-before pictures of the BEST BAND IN THE WORLD with like-minded people… what more could a man want! Derek was an absolute gent and the stories were great.
Spencer Hyland

We attended the exhibition and found the atmosphere warm and the pictures wonderful. For an old Jam fan like me, it was lovely to experience the feeling that the pictures brought about. I was at three of the gigs featured in the exhibition and it made me feel quite emotional. We had a chat with Derek and a couple of complimentary beers. My partner said it was the best thing about the Xmas period, so a big thank you for the invitation. There was always a common bond between the fans at Jam gigs and the exhibition brought back that feeling.
Rob Smith

We all had a great time, thanks so much for the invite and for sharing your wonderful pictures.
Cherrie Leanest

They always were my favourite set of pictures of The Jam. They made a great statement of where The Jam were at the time. Every book or record that featured a picture from that shoot made me want to see more. Thanks, Derek.
James Chapman

It was great to see some excellent images of THE best band in the world. It bought back some great memories from my distant youth. The whole event was extremely well put together with a really friendly atmosphere.
John Pointing

Derek's 'Absolute Luck' exhibition was an amazing insight into his wonderful experiences meeting and photographing The Jam!
Nick Gardiner

Some of the finest photos of one of England's most vital bands, presented to a room of like-minded souls. I will always support anyone's efforts to raise a glass to my band, our band, The Jam. Whole-hearted thanks to all those who contributed to this special event. Bring on the book!
Dave Newman

Great exhibition, Derek. Thanks so much for the invite, loved it!
Tony Egan

We thought the exhibition was excellent. Derek's a top bloke. Nice relaxed atmosphere with some great music and brilliant photographs! Loved all of it!
Jamie Smith

Great exhibition; I would have loved to have seen even more of Derek's photos of the Fab 3! The pictures bought back some great memories and there were definitely a few conversations starting with 'I remember'!
Paul Digby

I enjoyed the exhibition. It was very interesting, there was a good mix of pictures and they did a great job of showing the moments of Derek's beloved band that may have been forgotten if not for these wonderful photos. Nice work!
Asta Volkauskiene

The photos really capture the essence of the time and the band. No nonsense, no smiles and plenty of attitude.
Gordon Henman

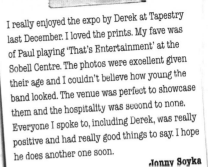

I really enjoyed the expo by Derek at Tapestry last December. I loved the prints. My fave was of Paul playing 'That's Entertainment' at the Sobell Centre. The photos were excellent given their age and I couldn't believe how young the band looked. The venue was perfect to showcase them and the hospitality was second to none. Everyone I spoke to, including Derek, was really positive and had really good things to say. I hope he does another one soon.
Jonny Soyka

The exhibition was amazing. Since I was 13, The Jam has been a major part of my life and Derek's fantastic photographs captured an important period for me. The pictures of the gigs brought back memories of the excitement of seeing the greatest band this planet has ever known. This was a time when bowling shoes, image and attitude were essential ingredients and just as crucial as the songs that have become ingrained in our psyche!
Richard Elby

It was like walking back into my old bedroom! The walls at the exhibition displayed many of Derek's great live shots; one that stood out was of Paul and Bruce singing into the same microphone and like the photographer said, 'Very Lennon & McCartney'. (*Note from Derek: I can't take credit for the comment, it was Alan's idea!*)
Phil Potter

My life connected to the music industry began with my first experience of a live gig at Wembley in December 1982. I was 14 and they were The Jam. An incredible night that could not be put into words. I thought every concert by every artist from then on would be the same, but of course it wasn't. To see a photo that had never seen the light of day from that same week at Wembley in '82 was the highlight of a brilliant exhibition. If I had one complaint, I was just gutted that despite being a friend of the photographer, I STILL drew a blank in the raffle…
Paul Dimmock

And from some of those involved . . .

Only 30 years in the making but well worth the wait! I remember Del Boy's excitement leading up to the event and the huge smile on his face when he greeted me... Great images taken by a fan who had fairly limited access but still achieved excellent results. Great choice of venue to show off these remarkable images. Congratulations to Derek and everyone involved with 'Absolute Luck'.

Jon Abnett

It was amazing to see the wonderful job that everyone involved did to bring 'Absolute Luck' to fruition. It was delightful to see how well received and appreciated Derek's Iconic Jam images were, and a joy to see Derek's face truly light up with delight, pride and wonder at the interest shown. It was also a revelation to see the impact a band like The Jam have had on the 600 people I met at the exhibition.

I'm very glad Derek has returned to photography as it gives him such obvious pleasure, and it is something that he seems to have a great eye for.

Krissie D'Souza

The iconic pictures taken by Derek of The Jam that day in 1981 in Chiswick Park for the *Absolute Beginners* shoot have become legendary among Jam fans throughout the world. Those pictures of Paul, Bruce and Rick would not look out of place in a Beatles book. Sharp blue suits, Weller in his psychedelic Lennon glasses and all three with confidence and attitude from being Britain's number one band.

As a 14-year-old schoolboy studying every detail of the *Absolute Beginners* single cover, the name Derek D'Souza conjured up the image of a top Anglo-Italian fashion photographer. Over 30 years later, when our paths crossed for the first time, I was delighted to discover there was no artistic attitude. Not only is Derek a great and very generous photographer, he was also 'one of us', a fan who I am honored to call a friend.

Guy Helliker

Gone are the days when a fan could get the chance to fulfill his dream. This happened to Derek and to see his face when Soho was adorned with his work is something I will always remember.

It was a complete pleasure to help curate this wonderful exhibition. Everyone involved had the same vision – to make this fun and show Derek's amazing photographs in the best light. It is one experience that I will never forget!

Alan Patterson

The 'Absolute Luck' showcase we held at Tapestry was a very exciting experience. I have known Derek for several years and so I suspected the event was going to be full of energy and love. What I didn't realise was how passionate he felt about photography and his obvious pride and desire for his pictures of The Jam to be displayed in the best way possible. With the added help of Alan and Emily working tirelessly in the background, we were all very proud that Tapestry held such a great exhibition.

Tony Garrett

I hadn't been working at Tapestry long when I was introduced to both Derek and Alan, and was really excited when I was told about the project. The 'Absolute Luck' exhibition was so much fun and I'm delighted to have been a part of it. It was an experience I will never forget. When's the next?!

Emily Green

I suppose on this occasion I do get to have the final word!

Well, we did it! What started as a crazy half-idea took shape, gathering speed, momentum and interest as word got around, until there was no stopping it. And finally, all that hard work by so many was worth it as we opened on 28th November 2012 and 'put up the closed sign' some three weeks later, just like the Man In The Corner Shop! While I have received many messages of support and congratulations, all greatly appreciated, please be under no illusion – this was 100% a team effort, and those involved should be immensely proud of what we achieved.

Special thanks to my lovely wife Krissie, who is full of ideas and ever willing to pitch in and help, a more supportive wife than any man could wish for; and to Al 'The Curator' Patterson, for his enthusiasm and excitement that spurred me on to get it done!

A massive thanks to the A-Team from Tapestry along with sterling support from 'The Curator', for the huge amount of effort and time they put into pretty much every aspect of the exhibition. This started with meetings to plan the event, right through to the time-consuming job of scanning and colour retouching my images so they would look their best; a huge task as the negatives and slides were over 30 years old and not much bigger than a large postage stamp. Their IT wizards worked their magic on the 'Absolute Luck' website, allowing us to manage the 600 guests over the 5 nights. The gallery area was repainted and the lighting adjusted to best display the images (the easels were a nice touch). All of the signage in the room was tastefully designed and beautifully printed and displayed alongside the images, which were mounted with laser precision (thanks Ed!) — they even managed to make my signature look good! The enlarged images in the front window were so striking, passersby would often stop to have a look or take pictures. In the two weeks prior to the exhibition launch I was on holiday in Florida, so a lot of the information was by email — apologies in particular to Emily, Tony, Alan and Jon for the amount of email — but you know I just wanted it to be 'right'. Somehow they managed to do all of this while still finding time to carry out their day jobs. The whole process was carried out with the utmost professionalism and enthusiasm and the team made it enjoyable and fun the entire time. Special mentions go to Emily Green for doing so much and then finding the time and energy to do more, and always with a smile; Tony Garrett for being the calm at the eye of the storm, for his attention to detail and for making sure my images looked the best they could be, and also for one of the funniest moments of the exhibition — at the end of the first night, we decided to swap around two prints, no. 5 and no. 13, with Tony describing the latter as "dull as dishwater" while I stood there right next to him! Alan, for doing so much when I could not be there in person, and for making sure it would be alright on the night. HUGE THANKS to Jess, Rich, Siobhan (hey bartenders!) for working All Day and All of the Night; also Craig, Keith, Joe, Brendan, Martin, Steven, Steve and Ed for all their good work, and I must also mention Lizzie May, the nicest person with a wicked sense of humour. My sincere apologies if anyone got missed. I truly could not have picked a more professional team to host my first exhibition and the venue in the heart of Soho was perfect (parking spaces and traffic wardens aside!).

Jon Abnett for suggesting and then helping to put together, lay out and organise the printing of the exhibition catalogue (which started as a photoshop prank by Jon), all while I was 5,000 miles away, AND for getting us mentioned on PW.com; Guy Helliker for being among the first to offer to help, for linking us to From The Jam's website, and for writing the coolest comments, David Coombs – a great photographer and great bloke – I reckon David Watts should have been David Coombs!; Eva Dussoy and Bill Johnson for putting together the website we desperately needed in double-quick time, Mamta Jamieson for immediately offering to help and for getting things done in the short time available; Lucy Philpot for a great turnout from EMI Music, and special thanks to NME for linking us on their website and for displaying the gallery images.

Finally, a massive thanks to everyone who came along and made it a special event, especially as it was so personal for me. A great mixture of family, friends, work colleagues, media and music business people, and last but not least, fellow fans of The Jam. Thanks also to those who could not make it but supported with words of encouragement.

We had an amazing five-night stint at Tapestry spread over three weeks, and were pretty much fully subscribed most nights.

It's true I can get by with a little help from my friends.

THANKS!

x

Derek

Tapestry were delighted to be asked by photographer and longterm friend of the company, Derek D'Souza, to help orchestrate his Exhibition of unseen and unpublished images of The Jam.

With our in-house scanning facilities and high end retouchers, we produced a seamless display of over twenty images, on a variety of different substrates.

From our London based offices in Soho, Highgate and Islington, we provide the following services:

- Advertising Production
- Colour Management
- Brand Identity
- Creative Artwork
- Design Implementation
- Packaging Pre-press
- Template Origination and Hosting
- Scanning
- Creative Retouching
- CGI
- Merchandise Visualisation
- Digital Media
- Asset Management
- Online and Mobile Content Development

- Workflow Automation
- Photographic and Fine Art Print
- Print Installation and Commissioning
- Wide Format Print Mounting and Finishing
- Moving Image Capture and Editing
- Managed Photographic Services
- Still Life and Location Photography
- Video Photography
- Retail and P.O.S
- Print Consultancy and Management
- Publishing Pre-media

Absolute Luck

TAPESTRY

THE COMPLETE PRODUCTION AGENCY.

Websites:

www.absoluteluck.co.uk
www.blinkandyoumissit.com
www.paulweller.com
www.fromthejam.co.uk
www.thejamfan.net
www.tapestry.co.uk
www.rcv-lille.com
www.zani.co.uk
www.heavysoul45s.co.uk

Gone but never forgotten:

My dear mum, Sarah Kent, John Weller, Dave Liddle

Other photos:

Dave Coombs – All 'Absolute Luck' Exhibition Photos (pages 161–163)
Suzanne Krasnowska – Derek and *Absolute Beginners* Poster (page 110)

Acknowledgements:

This book is the culmination of choices taken, decisions made and friendships forged, some of which will last a lifetime. Apart from the names mentioned, there are many others who have had an impact on my life. I could not name them all here for want of space, but many have influenced me in one way or another, and I want to thank them all for their love, friendship and support over the years.

Krissie D'Souza – for love and support, and for providing the 'piece of toast from the one you love most'. Jon Abnett for his patience, guidance and creative flair, and also for getting the ball rolling. Marshall Cavendish, starting with Chris Newson for picking up the ball and running with it before handing it on to Melvin Neo for the second half of the journey, and Stephanie Yeo for her eye for detail, combined with her professional and helpful manner.

Tony Garratt, Emily Green, Richard Wood, Jessica Pointing, Siobhan Cleary, Connor Jones, Craig Ralph, Keith Green, Lizzie May, Joe Shorter, Stephen Mason, Steven Butler, Steven Kemp and all the guys at Tapestry, not just for the high number of negatives and slides that had to be scanned and retouched which was a huge piece of work, but for their enthusiasm, professionalism and for breathing new life into old images while giving them true care and attention, and for making it so much fun!

Alan 'The Curator' Patterson, my partner in 'Absolute Luck', for restoring belief in not just my images but also my photography and myself. Stuart Deabill and Ian Snowball for paving the way with *Thick As Thieves*. Mark 'Bax' Baxter at Mono Media for his enthusiasm and support in his unique style. Delicious Junction for sponsorship and for THE sharpest shoes (did I mention I am a size 11?). Sir Eon Ballinger from London Calling Radio Station (RCV 99FM) for his enthusiasm and for the messages that always make me smile. Adam Cooper @ Heavy Soul Fanzine. Guy 'truly the nicest Guy' Helliker for always offering to help BEFORE he is asked, and for links on the FTJ site. Donna Ryan for looking after 'That Bag' with all of my Jam slides and negatives and for putting me at ease by telling me it was 'lost'! Mamta Jamieson for keeping her promises and for always being happy to help, Eva Bussey and Bill Johnson for the Absolute Luck website and so much more. David Coombs for his great photos that captured the atmosphere of the 'Absolute Luck' Exhibition.

The 'Eagle Eye' award for smoothing out the bumps in the text is shared between Stephanie Yeo, Ann Ledgard, Sophie Kimber and Krissie D'Souza. Donnie Munday for sharing his own prized possessions. Tony Egan for his words of support and encouragement when I really needed them, and for showing what really can be achieved when you put your mind (and back) into it. Den Davis for exciting events still to come! The Spitfires, DC Fontana, Louise Turner, The Brompton Mix and The Strypes for showing that the musical future is still bright!

To my Mum and Dad for everything, my global family (both actual and extended – special mentions to the D'Souza, Castelino, Menon, Fernandes, Athayd, Philpot and Meagher families), friends (again too many to mention, but a shout out to the following families: Ness, Hirons, Franks, Howlcroft, Warner, Malone, Brewer and Deering, for love, support and friendship.

To my work colleagues past and present, and to my fellow Jam Fans, special mentions to: Peter Deering, Paul Windmill, Sarah Kent, Suzanne Krasnowska, Melissa Cowell, Tony Porter, Christine Channon, Mick 'The Mod' Hughes, Pete Steadman, Vic Falsetta (and The Falsettas!), Pete & Steve Carver, Phil & Justine Potter, Stephen 'Meds' Medlin, Duncan Moreton, Paolo and Matteo Sedazzari, Russell Hastings, David 'Lofty' Lockhart, Gina Giraffe, Carl Grisley, Simon Franklin, Simon Korllang, Mark Tumplin, Gavin Frankland, Simon Kelly, Jay Hutchinson, Tim Lawrence and Andy Brown.

Last but not least, special thanks to Paul, Bruce and Rick, and to John and Ann Weller – for being a huge part of my life and without whom none of this would ever have happened.